BRIEF INSIGHTS ON MASTERING BIBLE DOCTRINE

Also by Michael S. Heiser

Brief Insights on Mastering the Bible

Brief Insights on Mastering Bible Study

BRIEF INSIGHTS ON MASTERING BIBLE DOCTRINE

80 Expert Insights,
Explained in a Single Minute

60-SECOND SCHOLAR SERIES

MICHAEL S. HEISER

ZONDERVAN

Brief Insights on Mastering Bible Doctrine

This title is also available as a Zondervan ebook.

Requests for information should be addressed to:
Zondervan, *3900 Sparks Dr. SE, Grand Rapids, Michigan 49546*

Library of Congress Cataloging-in-Publication Data

Names: Heiser, Michael S., author.
Title: Brief insights on mastering Bible doctrine : 80 expert insights on the Bible, explained in a single minute / Michael S. Heiser.
Description: Grand Rapids, MI : Zondervan, [2018] | Series: 60-second scholar series | Includes bibliographical references.
Identifiers: LCCN 2017054510 | ISBN 9780310566526 (softcover)
Subjects: LCSH: Bible--Study and teaching.
Classification: LCC BS600.3 .H44 2018 | DDC 220.071--dc23 LC record available at https://lccn.loc.gov/2017054510

Cover design and cover icon: Rick Szuecs Design
Interior design: Kait Lamphere

Printed in the United States of America

---

18 19 20 21 22 23 24 25 /DHV/ 15 14 13 12 11 10 9 8 7 6 5 4 3 2 1

To my divine council coconspirators:

Ronn Johnson, David Burnett, and Doug Vardell

CONTENTS

Introduction 15

Part 1. The Bible and Revelation

1. Are You a Splitter or a Joiner? 19
2. Don't Worry about Which Tradition Has the Right Canon .. 21
3. Minimizing the Bible's Human Authorship Undermines the Doctrine of Inspiration 23
4. Canonicity Is about God's Providence, Not Voting. 25
5. It's Bad Theology to Filter the Bible through Our Traditions .. 27
6. Your Bible Is and Isn't Inspired 29
7. General Revelation Is Important but Imprecise 31
8. You Can't Write about What You Can't Know 33
9. Any Doctrine of Biblical Inerrancy Depends upon Defining What "Error" Means 35
10. The Doctrine of Illumination Isn't a Promise That We'll Understand Scripture by Osmosis 37

Part 2. The Spiritual World

11. There Was No Rebellion of Angels before the Fall 41
12. Cosmic Geography Is a Biblical Concept 43
13. All Isn't One 45
14. Angels Image God Too 47
15. "God of Gods" Means Exactly What It Says 49

16. Israelites Knew That the Gods of the Nations Were Real . 51
17. Angels Don't Have Wings 53
18. Sometimes "Satan" Is Not the Devil 55
19. The Heavenly Host Does More than Sing around God's Throne like It Was a Camp Fire 57
20. Jesus Believed in Guardian Angels 59

Part 3. The Church

21. John 6 Is Not about the Lord's Supper 63
22. The Communion Table Isn't a Confessional Booth 65
23. What Was Paul Thinking When He Compared Baptism and Circumcision? 67
24. Motion or Meaning—What's More Important for Baptism? . . 69
25. Let's Not Confuse the Eternal State with the Canon 71
26. Sacraments or Ordinances—a Distinction Without a Difference? 73
27. Are Spiritual Gifts Natural Abilities or Divine Dispensations? 75
28. When the Twelve Apostles Died, Apostolic Authority Died with Them 77
29. The Baptism of the Holy Spirit Isn't about Speaking in Tongues. 79

Part 4. Israel

30. The Historic Covenants God Made with Israel Were Conditionally Unconditional 83
31. The Tower of Babel Is the Backdrop for the Old Testament Theology of Election 85

32. The Church Is a New Israel 87
33. The Promised Land: Forfeited, Fulfilled, or yet Future? .. 89
34. Israelite Circumcision Had Theological Meaning for Women 91
35. Israelites Were Forgiven through Animal Sacrifice in the Old Testament, but Those Sacrifices Did Not Atone for Many Kinds of Sin 93

Part 5. God: Father, Son, and Spirit

36. The Presence of the Holy Spirit with Believers in the Old Testament Was Occasional and Temporary 97
37. Jesus Wasn't God's Only Son 99
38. The Firstborn of All Creation Didn't Have a Beginning .. 101
39. The Holy Spirit Is Not an Impersonal Force 103
40. God Came to People as a Man before Jesus 105
41. God Neither Causes nor Needs Evil 107
42. The Humanity of Jesus Is as Important as His Deity 109
43. Jesus Is and Isn't God 111
44. Just as Jesus Is and Isn't God, the Spirit Is and Isn't Jesus ... 113
45. Just Because You Can't Grasp a Doctrine Doesn't Justify Denying That Doctrine 115
46. There Are Two Ways to Think about the Three Persons of the Godhead 117
47. Don't Assume the Doctrine of the Incarnation Is Easy to Grasp 119
48. God Was Never Dumb 121
49. God Won't Allow Human Evil or Ineptitude to Overturn His Plans 123
50. Jesus as God and Man: Addition or Subtraction? 125

51. Even Trinitarians Fight over the Trinity 127
52. God's Decrees and His Intentions Are Not Synonymous . . 129

Part 6. Human Nature

53. You Aren't a Body, Soul, and Spirit 133
54. Scripture Is Silent on the Origin of the Soul 135
55. The Image of God Refers to What We Are, Not Something Put into Us 137
56. God Is unlike Anything That Exists on Earth, except for Us . . 139
57. You're a Sinner Because You're Not God 141
58. Can Unbelievers Please God? 144

Part 7. Salvation

59. For by Grace You Are Saved through Faith Without Works Is Dead 149
60. No One Can Merit God's Favor 151
61. We Cannot Avoid Sinning, and We Contribute Nothing to Our Salvation 153
62. Without Sin There Is Innocence before God—and Eternal Life through the Resurrection of Christ 156
63. What Isn't Gained by Moral Perfection Can't Be Lost by Moral Imperfection 158
64. If You Believe, You Are Eternally Secure, and If You Don't, You Aren't 160
65. You Should Think Twice about Being More Offended by the Cross than God 163
66. Don't Fall for the False Dilemma Fallacy When You Think about the Atonement 165

67. Neither Being Poor nor Helping the Poor Are Tickets to Heaven 167
68. There's No Plan B When It Comes to Eternal Life 169
69. If You Are in Christ, Satan Has No Authority over Your Eternal Destiny 171
70. The Christian Life Is the Process of Becoming What You Are—and Will Be 173
71. You Don't Have Two of You inside Your Body 175
72. The Divine Presence of the Tabernacle and Temple Dwells inside Believers.................................. 179

Part 8. The Beginning and End of the World

73. Genesis 1:1–3 Allows for More than One View of Creation 181
74. The Original Created Earth Was Not Eden 183
75. The Bible Does Not Rule Out Death before the Fall 185
76. The Church Isn't Absent from the Book of Revelation... 187
77. Which Wrath Are We Talking About?................. 189
78. The Old and New Testaments Differ on the Details of the Afterlife, Not the Destinations 191
79. There's More than One Way to Understand Eternal Punishment 194
80. The Return of Jesus Was at Hand Two Thousand Years Ago—Just like It Is Now 196

INTRODUCTION

I know what you're thinking. What could be more mind-numbing than a book on Bible doctrine? I can think of lots of things more boring than Bible doctrine. Listening to NPR and watching golf come to mind. But that's just me. I'll admit that I'm fascinated by Bible doctrine because I'm nerdy. That's how I'm wired. But you think Bible doctrine is dreary because you've been conditioned. You equate reading about Bible doctrine with the waking trance that envelops you when you're on the phone waiting for a human customer service agent to break through the elevator music or, dare I say, when you're bored by the Sunday sermon. But here's the truth: sermons are boring because they don't get into doctrine.

Let me explain. Bible doctrine is ultimately about engaging your mind. Bible doctrine is what's produced by careful consideration of what the Bible says, what its stories imply, and what the behavior of its characters illustrates. If you're bored on Sunday morning, it's because you aren't being intellectually stimulated—you're being entertained or pacified. Thinking people know when they aren't being asked to think, and thinking Christians need engagement with Bible doctrine.

My goal in Brief Insights on Mastering Bible Doctrine is to awaken you (and not always gently) to how provocative and intriguing Bible doctrine can be. Think of it this way. Few Christians get into animated discussions about the songs selected for worship, the screen visuals, or the announcements. But when it comes to what "our church believes" (i.e., doctrine), many believers get pretty energetic about their voice being heard. Brief Insights on Mastering Bible Doctrine delivers eighty discussion-starters that will hopefully generate more light than heat.

There's a lot to think about in the Bible. We believe things on the basis of what it says, but the Bible doesn't spell everything out with equal clarity. What it says requires probing questions and mature reflection. Those are good exercises. Bible doctrine is the byproduct. It's what happens when we think about what the Bible says. How could that possibly be boring?

PART 1

THE BIBLE AND REVELATION

CHAPTER 1

Are You a Splitter or a Joiner?

I remember the events of 9/11 distinctly. I watched as much of the television coverage as I could. I read through dozens of accounts of the awful tragedy. Each one was filled with eyewitness testimony that recalled how planes rammed the towers of the World Trade Center and the pandemonium that ensued when the skyscrapers collapsed. Hundreds of newspapers would recount the tragic stories of lost loved ones and life-or-death heroism.

And yet, despite the fact that the world's attention was riveted on the attack, no two accounts of the events of those stories are the same. They all differ on the details. The reason is obvious. Each eyewitness recollects specific things. The fact that none of the stories agree doesn't mean in principle that any of them are wrong. They're just different.

How strange it is that people so often say that disagreements between biblical stories told more than once shows the Bible is unreliable. For example, there are instances in the Gospels where one gospel writer has two people in a scene with Jesus but another has one more or one less. *Contradiction!* Not exactly. In most cases, harmonizing disagreements between stories isn't difficult or unreasonable. And because of the familiarity we have with being exposed to multiple reports of the same event, the impulse to put them together in harmony is quite normal.

The issue of harmonizing passages that disagree is actually of profound theological importance. There are many descriptions of the second coming of Jesus in the New Testament, as well as Old Testament passages about the arrival of the Messiah at the end of the age. They don't all agree on all the details. For example, 1 Thessalonians 4:15–18 has the Lord meeting believers in the air when he comes back. Zechariah 14:4–5, however, has the Messiah returning to earth and setting foot on the Mount of Olives. The same passage in 1 Thessalonians has believers being caught up to be with the Lord in the air. Revelation 19:11–16 has Jesus returning on a white horse with an army.

Christians over the centuries have disagreed on how to approach these disagreements. Many opt to harmonize the accounts, to join them together into a grand portrayal of a *single* event: the second coming. Others, however, prefer to keep them separate, splitting up the descriptions of the Lord's return into two events—the removal of believers (living and dead) from the earth (the "rapture") and the second coming. Whether you're a splitter or a joiner depends on an interpretive *decision* you make. Neither is self-evident in the biblical text.

CHAPTER 2

Don't Worry about Which Tradition Has the Right Canon

The word "canon" refers to the Bible's collection of inspired books. It comes from a Greek word (*kanōn*) that refers to a rule or standard. For example, in Galatians 6:16, where Paul refers to "all who walk by this rule," the word translated "rule" is *kanōn.*

Christian traditions have historically disagreed on the canon. The Protestant canon—the one familiar to evangelical Christians—has thirty-nine and twenty-seven books in the Old and New Testaments respectively. The canon of Roman Catholicism agrees with that of Protestantism with respect to the New Testament but embraces more books in its Old Testament. Protestants refer to those "extra" books as the apocrypha, while Roman Catholics prefer the term deutero-canonical (literally, "second canon") to highlight their sacred status. The canons of Greek Orthodox Christians, Syriac Christianity, and the Ethiopian Church differ with both the Protestant and Roman Catholic canons. The Greek Orthodox canon includes books like 3–4 Maccabees, while the Ethiopian Church considers 1 Enoch canonical.

The Protestant Old Testament canon is based on those books that most (but not all) ancient Jews considered sacred. The Roman Catholic canon aligns closely with the books included in the Septuagint, the Greek translation of the Old Testament.

The Septuagint was the Bible of the earliest church because it was written in Greek, a language everyone could read in the ancient Mediterranean in the era of the apostles and their immediate successors.

So who's right? The honest answer is that no one knows for sure. Frankly, the uncertainty isn't something we need to care much about. Even if everyone agreed on the same list of books there would be theological and interpretive disagreements. That's obvious given the fact that there are dozens of denominations and sects *within* the Protestant tradition. In other words, agreeing on the canon is no guarantee of interpretive or theological harmony.

What we know from the ancient situation that led to debates over the canon is simple and clear. Early Christians—including converts from Judaism—read a wide range of books with important theological content. Some of those books never made it into any canon, yet prophets or apostles quote from them or allude to them in the books they produced. That tells us that whether their contemporaries thought a book was sacred or not didn't stop a biblical writer from reading it and using it to articulate theological truth. We ought to follow their example and read what they found useful so we can understand the material in whatever canon we embrace.

CHAPTER 3

Minimizing the Bible's Human Authorship Undermines the Doctrine of Inspiration

Christians believe in the inspiration of the Bible—that it has a supernatural origin. The idea comes from several passages, but the most familiar is probably 2 Timothy 3:16, which says that Scripture is "God-breathed." The Bible therefore has a divine origin and is of divine quality. But that idea can be carried too far—to the point where people don't recognize that the Bible is also the product of many human hands. Making that mistake actually undermines the idea of inspiration.

The reason is simple. The Bible bears the marks of its human writing process. Refusing to acknowledge them would make God seem awfully sloppy or confused. We need to instead embrace human authorship, realizing that God is the ultimate source of Scripture because it was he who chose the hands that would produce the Bible. It was God who led each writer along the path of life, molding him through every circumstance, bringing him to the time and place where the training, talents, and cumulative life experience had providentially prepared him to write whatever it was that God wanted written.

There are telltale signs of human activity in the Bible that make little sense if Scripture was downloaded into a passive author's brain.

The books of the Bible were not dictated by God, nor are they the product of "paranormal" silliness such as automatic writing, where an unseen being moves the hand and fingers across a page. The Bible is not a divine book; it is a divine human book. Both elements must be affirmed because they are taught in Scripture (2 Peter 1:20–21).

For example, we have four Gospels. Matthew, Mark, and Luke often overlap with respect to what they include about the life of Jesus. But they frequently have events in different order. The dialogue isn't always the same. And when you penetrate beyond the English, things like word choice, verb tense, grammatical person and number also vary in the compositions of the same events. This makes no sense at all if the Spirit dictated the content—he would look like a practical joker or, worse, a deity seeking to confuse the poor souls (us) who'd be reading the material, believing it came from an orderly divine mind.

Rather than being dictated or downloaded, books of the Bible were edited for coherence (e.g., the switches in person and number in Ezek. 1:1–3). Their content was deliberately arranged (e.g., Psalm 119, an acrostic featuring groups of eight verses that begin with successive letters of the Hebrew alphabet). The writers have specific agendas (e.g., 90 percent of John's Gospel is unique). None of these things are accidental, and none of them make sense if we minimize (or eliminate) the humanity of Scripture.

CHAPTER 4

Canonicity Is about Providence, Not Voting

In my years of teaching the Bible and theology, one topic that always seemed to give students anxiety was the doctrine of the Bible's canonicity. If the term is unfamiliar, *canonicity* refers to the *canonical* status of a book—that is, whether a given ancient book was deemed inspired and, therefore, should be included in the *canon*, the collection of books that we now call the Bible. Consequently, canonicity concerns how the books of the Bible were recognized as inspired.

This question can only be discerned historically, as there's no prophecy in the Bible that reveals what its contents would ultimately be. We know from history how the canon was recognized and that there were disagreements. But these historical events must also be processed theologically.

The historical events I'm referring to are not church councils, but historical records indicating what believing communities (Jewish or Christian) thought about their sacred books at various junctures. Yes, there were councils at which such matters were discussed, but they occurred in the wake of much more widespread engagement. Ancient documents provide evidence for an ongoing and active discussion over which books were inspired. For example, how writers quote and mention certain books can show us whether they thought those books were the word of God. We have access to early lists of sacred books along with commentary about the books that were debated.

It often disturbs people that there were debates about whether certain books were canonical. It shouldn't. One either believes providence is real, or not. If those who claim to follow Christ don't believe that the unseen hand of God is behind the acts and events of men—what we call history—then how serious can one's faith be in regard to the Bible's teaching about salvation? The reality of God and what God can do (and does) is not fragmented into truths and "less true truths." Men didn't debate, write, or hold meetings of which God wasn't aware, or at which he was absent. *God was in the process*.

A providential view of canonicity looks at all the back-and-forth among writers and thinkers as God directed the discussion to where it needed to go. The Spirit guided people to think well and thereby recognize the sacred, inspired nature of a book. Even in the wake of disagreement, the various Christian traditions recognize almost all the same books of the canon. The percentage of agreement *against* certain books is just as high. The fact that there is disagreement is important testimony that the canon *wasn't* just voted on by some clandestine, conspiratorial elite.

CHAPTER 5

It's Bad Theology to Filter the Bible through Our Traditions

Anyone interested in Bible study, from the new believer to the biblical scholar, has heard (and probably said) that if you want to correctly interpret the Bible, you have to interpret it *in context*. I'm certainly not going to disagree. But what exactly does that mean? Just what context are we talking about?

As Christians, whether consciously or otherwise, we've been trained to think that the history of Christianity is the true context for interpreting the Bible. It isn't. That might be hard to hear, but it's true. It's also obvious when you think about it.

The proper context for interpreting the Bible is not, for example, the church fathers. They lived a thousand years or more after most of the Old Testament was written. Less than a half dozen of them could read Hebrew. The New Testament period was a century or more removed from important early theologians like Tertullian and Irenaeus. Augustine, arguably the most famous early church figure, lived three hundred years *after* the conversion of Paul. More time has elapsed since the founding of the United States!

The farther down the timeline of history one moves, the greater the contextual gap becomes. The proper context for interpreting the biblical text is not the Catholic Church. It is not the rabbinic movements of late antiquity and the Middle Ages. It is not the

Reformation (Luther, Calvin, Zwingli, or the Anabaptists). It is not the Puritans. It is not evangelicalism in any of its flavors. *It is not the modern world at all.*

So what is the proper context for interpreting the Bible? Here's the transparently obvious truth I was talking about: the proper context for interpreting the Bible is the context of the biblical writers—the context that *produced* the Bible. Every other context is alien or at least secondary. The biblical text was produced by men who lived in the ancient Near East and Mediterranean between the second millennium BC and the first century AD. To correctly understand what a biblical writer wrote, we need to read Scripture in *their* context, not impose later contexts on the text. *We need the biblical writers living in our heads.*

As obvious as this seems, there is a pervasive tendency in the believing church to filter the Bible through creeds, confessions, and denominational preferences. That's not a sinister thing. It can be a helpful thing. But *replacing* exegesis of the biblical text in *its original* context with one of these filters is deeply misguided. It was God's decision to prepare men throughout their lives, and then prompt them at a given time, in a given culture, and in a given place to produce Scripture. Deeming other contexts preferable for interpretation over the thought processes of the biblical writers in their world, with their worldview, is to presume God's choices were not optimal or desirable. That's a low view of providence and bad theology.

CHAPTER 6

Your Bible Is and Isn't Inspired

Anyone with a high view of Scripture will affirm the doctrine of inspiration, which claims that the Bible's origin is attributable to the activity of God. I would certainly affirm that. So what do I mean? I mean simply that inspiration refers to the result of the providential process of putting each biblical book into its final form—not to the *copying* of those books or their *translation*. That means the Bible on your lap, your table, or your mobile phone is the inspired Word of God in terms of its origin but isn't inspired with respect to its *particular* translation.

Believe it or not, Jesus and the apostles were in the same situation. The synagogue in Jesus's hometown of Nazareth, where Jesus read from Isaiah 61 at the beginning of his ministry (Luke 4:16–30) didn't have *the* original Old Testament. It had a copy, like dozens of other synagogues in Judea and the ancient Mediterranean. In most of the instances (scholars put it as high as 80 percent), when Jesus or a biblical writer quotes the Old Testament, the citation is not from the traditional Hebrew (Masoretic) text but from the Septuagint, a Greek translation. Nevertheless, they quote it as if it had the authority of the Word of God. It was no less inspired because it was a translation, yet everyone knew translations weren't the product of the process of inspiration.

Translations are the Word of God insofar as they accurately reflect the content of the original books of the Bible. To have any hope of doing that, translators must not only be skilled in their knowledge of the original languages of the Bible (Hebrew, Greek, and Aramaic), but they must be working from faithful copies of the original biblical books. Manuscripts of course disagree, but most divergences do not make it difficult to knowing which wording was more likely the original. Of course, no one can claim omniscience when it comes to the thousands of manuscripts of the Bible that have been recovered and carefully studied. But while certainty of the original text of the Bible isn't absolute, it is nevertheless unbelievably high.

At the end of the day, most English translations are trustworthy, especially modern ones that were produced by a team of scholars with multiple levels of review. Where those working on the translation encounter manuscript differences or places where more than one translation is possible, a good modern translation will notify the reader in footnotes. It is illogical, and demonstrates a low view of God's providence, to suggest that lack of perfection and omniscience means we don't really have the word of God.

CHAPTER 7

General Revelation Is Important but Imprecise

Most students of Bible doctrine are more familiar with the doctrine of inspiration than with revelation, and I'm not referring to the last book of the New Testament. The doctrine of revelation, however, is just as important as inspiration since it helps us understand why we need the Bible.

"Revelation" refers to that which has been revealed. That doesn't sound terribly profound, but when we consider God as the source of what's being revealed, this simple idea demands some reflection. On one hand, the doctrine of revelation is a study of how God chose to communicate with humanity and how we can know things about God. On the other hand, that topic opens the door to a lot of questions, including: Is the Bible the only valid revelation about God? If God uses sources other than the Bible to tell us about himself, are God's other means of communication supernatural? Are all his means equally clear?

Theologians like to distinguish two broad types of revelation related to what we can know about God: general revelation and special revelation. The Bible talks about both, but the Bible itself falls under the second category.

General revelation refers to what we can learn about God through our general experience of the world and can process with our five senses. In other words, it refers to our experience of nature. The fact that our world exists instructs us. The world either created itself, had no cause, or was brought into being by some power greater than itself. Philosophers and theologians over the course of millennia have shown the first two options to be logically incoherent. We are thus driven to option three: the world (and moreover, the universe) as we know it must have had a cause. Natural causes are unsatisfying because they raise the quandary of how the natural means of creating the universe came to be prior to the universe. The infinite regress of cause and effect this view requires never really answers the question. Consequently, an external, intelligent, intentional cause—God—has had the most explanatory power. We get all that just from observing who we are, where we are, and asking the obvious question of how it all got here.

Through creation we learn about God's "invisible attributes, namely, his eternal power and divine nature" (Rom. 1:20). We also get a glimpse of God's grandeur and power (Ps. 19:1), how our existence depends on his (Acts 17:28, 29), our accountability to him (Acts 17:30–31), and his goodness (Matt. 5:45). We may not learn the specifics of God's plan or the gospel, but general revelation is still an important teacher.

CHAPTER 8

You Can't Write about What You Can't Know

Earlier we talked about how some of what we know about God can be discerned through things we can know and experience. But general revelation offers limited instruction. While creation teaches us some crucial theology, there are a host of spiritual truths we can't learn from nature. General revelation must be augmented by special revelation.

Special revelation describes all God's communication with us besides creation. The term refers to the information God gives us that couldn't be gained from our experience of the universe he made.

The Bible is special revelation. God chose men and providentially prepared them throughout their lives for the occasions at which he prompted them, by his Spirit and sometimes by someone else's influence, to write something down for posterity. What they wrote is often quite normal, even knowable from other historical sources: battles, kings, bloodlines, stories, and maxims for living. But the biblical writers would not have known anything about who Jesus really was or why he was here without being taught by God or Jesus himself (Matt. 16:17; Luke 24:36–49).

The Bible is also our source for what goes on in the unseen realm, the domain of God. The spiritual world is utterly unknowable to human beings. Our existence is that of embodiment in the natural world created for us. We can know nothing of this alternative, parallel reality. Information about who God is, what he did before or at creation, what the heavenly host do in their service to him, and what happens when we pass from the natural realm to the spiritual world at death—all of this is naturally unknowable to us.

All of our knowledge about the spiritual realm must come from beings (e.g., God, angels) who reside there. The Bible has this knowledge dispensed through direct divine encounters (1 Sam. 3; Isa. 6; Ezek. 1; 10), dreams (Gen. 28:10–22; 1 Kings 3:1–15), visions (Dan. 8–9; 2 Cor. 12:1–4; 1 Kings 22:19–23), and angelic mediators (Dan. 8:17; 10:11, 16, 19; Rev. 10:9; 17:7, 15).

The lessons are straightforward. Humans cannot know the mind of God without God telling us what's on his mind. They cannot know what happens in the spiritual realm unless they are transported or given a supernatural vision. Though Scripture was produced through human beings under the providence of God, the writers were given information about the spiritual world and its activities that they couldn't have known otherwise. In that respect, special revelation transcends general revelation.

CHAPTER 9

Any Doctrine of Biblical Inerrancy Depends upon Defining What "Error" Means

Most Christians are accustomed to the reality that believers in Jesus Christ disagree on many points of doctrine. But in my experience, a lot of Christians seem surprised that the doctrine of inerrancy is among the areas of disagreement. The reason is that to agree on what inerrancy means requires agreeing on how to define what does or does not count as an error.

Defining what counts as an error isn't easy. Is the Bible allowed to use approximations? How much precision is necessary? Numbers 25:9 and 1 Corinthians 10:8 describe the same event, but the numbers employed disagree. According to 2 Chronicles 4:2, the diameter of the "molten sea" was 10 cubits and the circumference 30 cubits. Since we know that the circumference of a circle is π (3.14159) times the diameter, if the molten sea was indeed circular, the math doesn't add up precisely. Are normative, naked eye observations that aren't scientifically correct to be considered errors (e.g., "when the sun had risen, they went to the tomb"; Mark 16:2)? Does it matter if biblical writers held unscientific ideas, common in their day? Some say yes, others no.

While Christians have debated inerrancy for many years, divergence among Christians over the idea came into more pronounced focus beginning in the sixteenth century, the Age of Exploration. European explorers, for example, crossed the Atlantic for the first time. They discovered people and places the Bible didn't mention. If everyone had been wiped out by the flood except for Noah and his family, how did people in North and South America come from Noah's sons? Things got even more complicated when the languages and literatures of ancient India, Egypt, and Mesopotamia were, respectively, deciphered and translated. Suddenly, competing accounts of human civilizations and chronologies emerged, and the physical remains of these ancient peoples had to be taken into account. The Bible was no longer the only ancient record of the distant human past. The nineteenth century would produce Darwinism; the twentieth, the disruption of Newton's "clockwork universe" in modern physics. Today, the inerrancy debate includes knowledge sources like genetics and neuroscience.

Christian thinkers and biblical scholars have approached such difficulties from a wide range of trajectories, which in turn has produced a spectrum of positions on inerrancy. But that's the point: people have picked positions that make sense to them, and not everyone agrees on what makes sense. Whatever your definition, realize that differences of opinion on something like inerrancy arise not from hard hearts but from real issues.

CHAPTER 10

The Doctrine of Illumination Isn't a Promise That We'll Understand Scripture by Osmosis

I do a lot of blogging about biblical studies. I've been at it now for seven years. In that span of time I've come to the conclusion that the first part of John 16:13 contains one of the most misunderstood and abused statements in the Bible: "When the Spirit of truth comes, he will guide you into all the truth." This passage is a refuge for anyone who wants to disagree with what someone else says in defense of their own view. And when engagement with someone else would require serious work, or more training in things like biblical language study, the statement does double duty as an excuse not to make the effort. It's as though people look at John's words and presume that the Spirit will simply impress a passage's meaning onto their brain if they've prayed to know what it means.

The absurdity of this idea is painfully obvious. The fact that someone is a believer is no guarantee that all believers will look the same way at the same passage. Not all Christians agree on how a given verse or passage should be interpreted, yet they all have the Holy Spirit. Since the apostolic era ended, sincere, holy, and gifted Christians have disagreed on how to understand what the New Testament says (not to mention the Old Testament). Yet folks appeal to this verse as though its meaning is self-evident.

John 14:26 gets pressed into the same service: "But the Helper, the Holy Spirit, whom the Father will send in my name, he will teach you all things and bring to your remembrance all that I have said to you." Both this passage and John 16:13 are unfortunately ripped from their own context. Both selections from the Gospel of John focus on the notion that when Jesus was no longer on the earthly scene, the Spirit would help the disciples remember what Jesus had taught them. The Gospels bear witness to the fact that the Spirit did indeed do that. We have the proof in those four accounts of Jesus's life and teachings. But on what basis would we conclude that the verses mean that the Spirit would implant the meaning of any given passage that is written in the Bible into the minds of believers? The verse simply doesn't make that claim.

John 16:13 hints at what illumination really means. The Spirit guides us, which implies that we are moving somewhere, doing something, making an effort to understand the truth in Scripture. Discerning the right interpretation of a passage (or one that could survive critique) is not a passive activity. You don't learn doctrine (or anything else) by osmosis. Proximity to the Bible and the Spirit's indwelling presence doesn't mean that correct understanding just drifts into your consciousness via either source. The Spirit will direct your thinking only when you're thinking, and that requires study. Don't expect a doctrine download. It isn't coming.

PART 2

THE SPIRITUAL WORLD

CHAPTER 11

There Was No Rebellion of Angels before the Fall

The study of angels ("angelology") is one of the more popular topics in Bible doctrine. It's also one of the most vulnerable to misunderstanding. Part of the reason is that the fascination with angels never seems to subside. Even today there are plenty of television shows and movies that frame the way many people think about them. But some myths about angels aren't contemporary ones. We can't blame everything on Hollywood.

One of the more persistent misconceptions in Christian angelology is that there was a war in heaven before the fall, perhaps even before the creation of humanity, that led to the defection of one-third of the angels to the dark side. Satan, many are taught, was the leader of this heavenly rebellion.

The problem with this idea is that it is nowhere taught in the Bible. The closest one comes is Revelation 12:3–4a, 7–9:

> And another sign appeared in heaven: behold, a great red dragon, with seven heads and ten horns. . . . His tail swept down a third of the stars of heaven and cast them to the earth. . . . Now war arose in heaven, Michael and his angels fighting against the dragon. And the dragon and his angels fought back, but he was defeated, and there was no longer any

> place for them in heaven. And the great dragon was thrown down, that ancient serpent, who is called the devil and Satan, the deceiver of the whole world—he was thrown down to the earth, and his angels were thrown down with him.

This passage seems to say precisely what I'm saying isn't in the Bible. We have Satan (here, cast as "the dragon") and a third of the angels (stars) were cast down. But the passage is not what it seems. I purposefully omitted the second half of verse 4 along with verses 2 and 5. Revelation 12:2 describes a woman who is pregnant, about to give birth. After the dragon casts the stars to the earth, we read in Revelation 12:4b–5:

> And the dragon stood before the woman who was about to give birth, so that when she bore her child he might devour it. She gave birth to a male child, one who is to rule all the nations with a rod of iron, but her child was caught up to God and to his throne.

The "war in heaven" scene of Revelation 12 is therefore clearly connected to *the birth of the Messiah*, and even that quite obviously comes after the creation of humanity and the fall. The Bible never tells us about a mass primeval rebellion of angels.

CHAPTER 12

Cosmic Geography Is a Biblical Concept

As Deuteronomy 32:8–9 refers back to the Tower of Babel incident, it frames the entirety of the biblical concept of the elect people of God. But that means it's also the point of reference for the nonelect status of everyone else. Election was about access to the truth about the true God, not salvation per se. Israel was to be the conduit through which the nonelect nations would be brought back into the family of the true God. The Israelites were a kingdom of priests.

This worldview produced what could be called cosmic geography—the idea that certain ground is holy while other ground is unholy, under the dominion of hostile spiritual beings. The land of Israel was holy because the presence of Yahweh, the true God, was there. Even before Israel occupied Canaan, God's presence moved with them through the wilderness. And the closer one got to the ark of the covenant, which was located at the center of the camp (Num. 2–3) in the most holy place within the tabernacle, the higher the degree of sanctity.

The concept explains many odd episodes in the Old Testament. The bizarre request of Naaman to take dirt from Israel back to his home country after he'd been healed of leprosy by Elisha suddenly makes sense. He now believed in Yahweh, and knew that Israel was holy ground (2 Kings 5). After God destroyed the statue of Dagon in the Philistine temple—where they had taken the ark of the covenant—the Philistine priests avoided walking on the spot where the incident had taken place (1 Sam. 5:5). They knew better. Yahweh had commandeered that space. When David found himself driven out of Israelite territory, he complained that he had been told to go worship other gods (1 Sam. 26:17–20). David wasn't denying God's omnipresence. He just knew he belonged in Israel. It was Yahweh's domain. Daniel 10 is even more explicit; there are cosmic princes over nations (Dan. 10:13, 20).

The New Testament presumes this cosmic-geographical worldview. It's why Paul's vocabulary for the evil spiritual powers of darkness is peppered with geographical rulership terms: *rulers* (1 Cor. 2:6; Eph. 3:10; 6:12; Col. 1:16), *authorities* (Eph. 3:10; 6:12; Col. 1:16), *thrones* (Col. 1:16), *dominions* (Col. 1:16).

Paul understood Deuteronomy 32:8–9. He also knew that it was through Israel and her messiah that those nations would be reclaimed (Gen. 12:3). As he put it in Acts 17:26–27, "[God] made from one man every nation of mankind to live on all the face of the earth, having determined allotted periods and the boundaries of their dwelling place, that they should seek God, and perhaps feel their way toward him and find him."

CHAPTER 13

All Isn't One

We live in a day when personal "spirituality" trumps commitment to any form of Christianity with deep historical roots. The latter is viewed as anything from quaint to closed-minded. Believing in something that holds to absolute truth claims and moral standards is considered backward, even dangerous. Truth evolves, we are told. We need to get with the times. Our experience should guide us toward what is true (at least what's true for us right now, anyway).

One of the more oft-repeated mantras that frame this approach to spiritual truth is that "all is one," an idea known by academics as *monism*. In more comprehensible terms, monism refers to the notion that all existing things share the same reality or substance. In terms of the world we experience or know through science, monism asserts that nothing exists outside of the created material world (or universe).

I hope you see the theological problem. If nothing exists outside material reality, then there is no separate Creator. God would have to be *in* creation in all its parts. There would be no distinction between Creator and creation. If all that exists is one and is a part of the material reality of the universe, then either God is part of creation, or he doesn't exist at all. If monism is true, he cannot stand apart from creation. And that's not all. If God is part of this "one reality," then we are God, in some sense, and he is us.

The Bible rejects these ideas. Scripture quite clearly teaches that all things that exist, visible or invisible, were created by an uncreated God (Gen. 1:1; John 1:1; Col. 1:16). God is not part of creation; he produced creation. He is not material; he is Spirit (Isa. 31:3; John 4:24). He is not us; we are not him (Gen. 1:26–27; 2:7).

This firm distinction between the Creator and creation is known as dualism. Whereas monism affirms *one* (Greek: *monos*) reality, the Bible affirms two (Greek: *duo*) realities: God and everything God created, which is everything else.

Whether or not we realize it, dualism is one of the most important theological ideas in the Bible. Without it, God is not the Creator, and we don't need redemption because there's no God to offend. It doesn't get any more fundamental than that.

CHAPTER 14

Angels Image God Too

We are created in God's image. To be created *in* God's image means to be created *as* God's image. We represent God on earth, a task we can accomplish by means of attributes given to us by God that make us like him. However, there is something in Genesis 1:26 that's important for a doctrinal understanding of God's heavenly host, members of the group that are commonly called angels:

> Then God said, "Let *us* make man in *our* image, after *our* likeness."

Many Bible students presume that the plural pronouns in this verse are cryptic references to the Trinity. If this verse were the only such passage that indicated divine plurality, that approach would be workable. But it isn't. As we'll discuss in the next chapter, Psalm 82 and other passages indicate that the members of the heavenly host are in view when such language occurs, and some of them are quite corruptible. The idea that God is talking to himself is flawed for the same reason: other passages use plurality language to speak of other divine beings in God's presence. Lastly, some interpreters suggest that the explanation is a grammatical phenomenon called the "plural of majesty," but in Hebrew this occurs only with nouns (the forms here are verbs). The answer is more straightforward than might appear, and it has an interesting theological payoff.

In Genesis 1:26 God speaks to a group; he announces his intention to create humankind to the members of his heavenly host (1 Kings 22:19; Ps. 89:5–8). When Genesis 1 describes the creation of humanity, there is no opposition from those who heard God's intention, and only God does the creating (the verbs of creation in Genesis 1:27 are grammatically *singular*). In fact, the language shifts from humanity being created in "our" image to God creating humankind in "his own image" (Gen. 1:27).

We use this sort of language every day. A suggestion like "let's go for a drive" illustrates what's going on well. One speaker announces an intention to a group. There is only one driver. The group (literally) goes along for the ride. They are passive participants.

While the members of God's host—or angels in nontechnical language—do not participate in creation, they in some sense are also God's imagers. Since the plural language shifts to the singular when the creating happens, it's clear that humans don't image (represent) angels. The plurality, then, must indicate that angels must also image their creator, just as we do. Both humans and angels are tasked with representing God, though the task happens in different realms, one visible, the other invisible. This makes sense in light of the very obvious fact that angelic beings also share attributes that God possesses, like intelligence and freedom.

Ultimately, the plural language in Genesis 1:26 tells us that God wants all his intelligent creations to represent him. As in heaven, so on earth.

CHAPTER 15

"God of Gods" Means Exactly What It Says

The special covenant name of God in biblical Hebrew is Yahweh. English translations mark it with LORD (spelled in small caps). The name is derived from the Hebrew verb *hayah*, which means "he is" or "I am" in the first person (Ex. 3:14). For faithful Israelites, Yahweh was "the God of gods" (Deut. 10:17), "the great king of all gods" (Ps. 95:3). How then do we strangely presume that the Israelites didn't believe other gods were real, that they were merely idols?*

Not only did the biblical writers believe that the other gods were real, but they said so in Scripture. Psalm 82:1 says, "God [*elohim*] has taken his place in the divine council; in the midst of the gods [*elohim*] he holds judgment." These plural *elohim* are mentioned again later in the psalm. God says to them,

> I said, "You are gods,
> sons of the Most High, all of you;
> nevertheless, like men you shall die,
> and fall like any prince." (Ps. 82:6–7)

---

* See Michael S. Heiser, *The Unseen Realm: Recovering the Supernatural Worldview of the Bible* (Lexham, 2015).

These *elohim* had become corrupt (Ps. 82:2–5) and the superior God of Israel was going to judge them.

The divine council of Psalm 82:1 is therefore not a group of men. Psalm 89:6–7 makes that crystal clear: "For who *in the skies* can be compared to the LORD [Yahweh]? Who among the heavenly beings ["sons of God"] is like the LORD [Yahweh], a God greatly to be feared in *the council of the holy ones*." We catch a glimpse of a council meeting in 1 Kings 22:19–23, where the heavenly host, called spirits, surround Yahweh and determine alongside him how wicked Ahab, who Yahweh sentenced to die, should meet his end.

That all sounds odd since we assign one set of unique attributes to the word G-O-D. Biblical writers didn't use *elohim* that way. That word is not used only of Yahweh but describes demons (Deut. 32:17), gods of various nations (1 Kings 11:33), the disembodied human dead (1 Sam. 28:13), and the divine beings of Yahweh's heavenly council (Ps. 82:1, 6). The term *elohim* therefore *cannot* point to one specific set of attributes. Rather, it's the term an Old Testament writer would use of any spirit being whose normal domain was the spirit world. For faithful Israelites, Yahweh was an *elohim*, but no other *elohim* was Yahweh. He was unique and incomparable. Yahweh is all powerful (Jer. 32:17, 27; Ps. 72:18; 115:3), the sovereign king over the other *elohim* (Ps. 95:3; Dan. 4:35), the creator of the heavenly host (Ps. 148:1–5; Neh. 9:6; cf. Job 38:7), and the lone *elohim* who deserves worship from the other *elohim* (Ps. 29:1).

Are we to conclude that God presides over nonexistent spiritual beings? That the God of Israel is "king of all beings that don't exist"? That's like saying "Yahweh is greater than all the Marvel super heroes." Big deal. They aren't real. That mocks God, and that is *not* what the biblical writers do.

CHAPTER 16

Israelites Knew That the Gods of the Nations Were Real

Everyone seems to know the Tower of Babel story. Far fewer know that Genesis 11:1–9 isn't the only version of that episode in the Bible. The other comes in Deuteronomy 32:8–9, arguably one of the most important passages in the Old Testament, and one of the most frequently overlooked.

> When the Most High apportioned the nations as an inheritance, when he divided up humankind, he established the borders of the peoples according to the number of the sons of God. But the LORD's portion is his people, Jacob his allotted heritage.

When God divided the nations, which was the punishment at Babel when the languages were confused, he distributed the nations among "the sons of God." Some Bible translations have "sons of Israel" instead of "sons of God." But *Israel didn't exist at the time of the Tower of Babel*. God only called Abraham and began the nation of Israel *after Babel* (Gen. 12). "Sons of Israel" can't be right. "Sons of God" is also what the Dead Sea Scrolls say, the oldest manuscripts of the Bible. The ESV has it right.

Deuteronomy 4:19–20 tells us more. God allotted other gods *to* the nations he dispersed at Babel. Taken together, these two passages tell us why the other nations worshipped other gods. Their false religion and alienation from the true God was a punishment from the Most High. But the punishment wasn't meant to last forever. When God called Abraham after Babel, he told the patriarch that through his offspring the other nations would be blessed. God had disinherited the nations but would allow them to find their way back to him. As Paul put it, God "determined allotted periods and the boundaries of [humanity's] dwelling place, that they should seek God, and perhaps feel their way toward him and find him" (Acts 17:26–27).

Unfortunately, the gods assigned by the God of Israel to the other nations became corrupt (Ps. 82). Instead of directing the nations to the true God, they seduced God's own portion, Israel (Deut. 17:1–3; 29:22–28; 32:17). This hostility and conflict frames the rest of the Old Testament—the story of Yahweh against the gods and Israel against the nations.

This conflict extends into the New Testament as well. Paul rarely uses the word "demons" to describe the spiritual opposition we face. He uses words like "principalities," "powers," "thrones," "dominions," and "authorities," all of which convey the idea of geographical rulership. The message is that the whole world is under the dominion of unseen powers of darkness, save for those who are in Christ. Babel explains why that is so.

CHAPTER 17

Angels Don't Have Wings

Angels fascinate people, both Christians and those of other faiths. There are millions of websites that discuss them. Try searching Amazon for the word "angel" or "angels" in book titles. There are over one hundred thousand of them. But despite the interest in angels, what people think the Bible teaches about them is often mythical.

Googling images of angels will tell you what I mean. Sorry, but angels don't have wings. While we're talking about searching, go ahead and find some Bible software or a website that lets you search all the words in the Bible. You won't find a single verse with angels and wings in it. The idea is a myth, pure and simple. The same goes for angels playing harps and singing 24/7. They do a lot more than that. Angels are members of God's heavenly host that deliver messages to people and help God run the affairs of human history (e.g., 1 Kings 22:19–23; Dan. 4:13, 17, 23–24; 7:10).

The idea of angels having wings comes from the flawed presumption that cherubim and seraphim are angels. They aren't. Cherubim and seraphim are never called angels in the Bible.

Unlike angels, which are always described with human forms (e.g., Gen. 18–19 [cf. 19:1, 10–12]; Judg. 6), cherubim are not. While cherubim have some human elements (e.g., hands), they are supernatural yet creaturely hybrids with multiple faces, feet like a calf, wings, and a glowing appearance like burnished bronze (Ezek. 1:4–14; cf. Ezek. 10:1–8, 20).

Seraphim are also otherworldly human-creature hybrids (Isa. 6:1–7). They have hands and feet, but also wings. The term "seraphim" is commonly thought to refer to its burning or glowing appearance (the Hebrew verb *saraph* means "to burn"), but the term actually derives from the noun *saraph* ("serpent"). Seraphim are luminous, serpentine beings with wings.

Images of cherubim and seraphim are well known from ancient cultures of the biblical period because the terms are borrowed from Mesopotamia and Egypt, respectively. In both cases these creatures were guardians of the divine throne, which aligns well with the contexts of Ezekiel 1 and Isaiah 6. Ezekiel was writing in Babylon, so the cherubim imagery made sense to his audience. The same can be said for Isaiah, as he ministered during the times of Uzziah and Hezekiah. These Judean kings were known to use Egyptian symbols in their royal iconography, and so his description of seraphim in Isaiah 6 would have been readily understood. Archaeologists have actually discovered the royal seal of Hezekiah, which was decorated with a winged scarab beetle.

A lot of what you think you know about angels comes from tradition, not the Bible. Our angelology needs to come from the biblical text.

CHAPTER 18

Sometimes "Satan" Is Not the Devil

The book of Job famously opens with a scene in God's courtroom: "Now there was a day when the sons of God came to present themselves before the LORD, and Satan also came among them" (Job 1:6). The conversation that ensues between God and "Satan" produces Job's terrible suffering. That's a seemingly straightforward account. But things aren't what they seem.

Most modern study Bibles will have a footnote at the word "Satan" in this verse that typically informs readers that the Hebrew term could be (and ought to be) translated "the adversary." The reason for this note is a well-known rule of Hebrew grammar. "Satan" in Job 1–2 is actually the phrase *ha-satan*. The word *ha* in Hebrew is the definite article, "the" in English. The second word is a noun that means "adversary." Like English, Hebrew grammar does not allow a proper personal name to be preceded by the definite article. I wouldn't refer to myself, for example, as "the Mike." This grammatical rule means that *satan* is *not* a proper personal name in Job 1–2. The figure in Job 1–2 is not God's archenemy known as Satan in the New Testament. In other words, the devil is not in Job 1–2. Consequently, wherever *ha-satan* occurs it should be translated "the adversary."

When *satan* is used without the definite article to describe a divine being, it could in theory describe an evil divine being, but it never does so in the Old Testament. Rather, it describes a divine being in God's service. For example, the word *satan* occurs in Numbers 22:22, where the angel of the Lord is described as serving as God's "adversary" against Balaam.

In Job 1–2, the *satan* (adversary) is a member of God's divine court. His job is clear: he roams the earth to see if humans were obeying God (Job 1:7). God takes the occasion to praise Job, at which point the adversary oversteps his authority. The adversary claims that God is ignorant of Job's character. The adversary asserts that Job's righteousness depends on God's blessing. He challenges God's knowledge and authority to correctly assess Job. That challenge is the key to the book's real purpose, which is a subject for another day.

Why does the New Testament, then, use *satan* as a proper name? The New Testament is written in Greek, and so there is no grammatical obstacle. More importantly, New Testament writers (and Jewish writers in the centuries leading up to the New Testament) saw the great enemy of Eden as "opposing" God's will and plan. Since cosmic and earthly rebellion began with him, he was viewed as the "adversary of adversaries," which led to the word *satan* being transformed into a proper name. There's no question the title is deserved.

CHAPTER 19

The Heavenly Host Does More than Sing around God's Throne like It Was a Camp Fire

In chapter 17, I wrote that heavenly beings help God run the affairs of human history. It's time to pick up that thread.

Recall that God's heavenly host is depicted as a council (Ps. 82:1). We get an intriguing glimpse of how council members participated in God's decisions in 1 Kings 22. The first fifteen verses tell us about a meeting between King Jehoshaphat of Judah, the southern Israelite kingdom, and the wicked King Ahab of Israel, the northern kingdom. Ahab wanted Jehoshaphat to join forces with him to attack Ramoth-gilead. Jehoshaphat wanted to hear from a prophet of Yahweh about the matter. Enter Micaiah, who let Ahab have it:

> And Micaiah said, "Therefore hear the word of the LORD: I saw the LORD sitting on his throne, and all the host of heaven standing beside him on his right hand and on his left; and the LORD said, 'Who will entice Ahab, that he may go up and fall at Ramoth-gilead?' And one said one thing, and another said another. Then a spirit came forward and stood before the LORD, saying, 'I will entice him.' And the LORD said to him, 'By what means?' And he said, 'I will go out, and will be a lying spirit in the mouth of all his prophets.' And

> he said, 'You are to entice him, and you shall succeed; go out and do so.'" (1 Kings 22:19–22)

Verse 20 tells us in no uncertain terms that God had decided it was time for Ahab to die. God then asked the host of heaven standing in attendance (called "spirits" in v. 21) *how Ahab's death should be accomplished*. The council members debated the matter until one of the spirit beings came forward with a proposition: "I will go out and I will be a false spirit in the mouth of all his prophets." Knowing this would work, God ordered the spirit to get the job done. The point is that God's heavenly host participates in God's rule. God decrees the end but can choose to allow free beings to decide the means.

The same participatory model is also discernible in Daniel 4, where Nebuchadnezzar tells Daniel about a dream he had that involved a huge tree and a watcher, which is a term for a divine being (a "holy one"; Dan. 4:13, 17, 23). In his dream, the watcher proclaimed that the tree would be chopped down, leaving only its stump. The tree and the stump are symbols for Nebuchadnezzar, who will lose his mind, the watcher announces, and become like an animal (Dan. 4:13–16). Daniel 4:17 then adds this detail:

> The sentence is by the decree of the watchers, and the decision by the command of the holy ones, in order that the living will know that the Most High is sovereign over the kingdom of humankind, and to whomever he wills he gives it.

Who issues the decree, God or the watchers? The answer is both, but credit for sovereign rule is given to God. God, of course, doesn't *need* a council, but he nevertheless uses his host in his rule. He doesn't need us either, but extends us the same privilege.

CHAPTER 20

Jesus Believed in Guardian Angels

Jesus's parable of the lost sheep is a Christian favorite. It teaches us about God's tenacious love to seek lost sinners who have gone astray. It's also easy to rehearse to children. But how many times have we told (or heard) the story minus the statement that immediately precedes it?

> See that you do not despise one of these little ones. For I tell you that in heaven their angels always see the face of my Father who is in heaven. (Matt. 18:10)

This statement—that children have an angel who intercedes for them before the Father or perhaps reports to God on their behalf—is the basis for the notion of guardian angels. It's amazing how many Christians dismiss an idea that Jesus so clearly affirms.

A dismissal of this doctrine is all the more absurd when we consider other statements about angels that pertain to adults. For example, the psalmist, speaking to those who trust in the Most High God says, "For he will command his angels concerning you to guard you in all your ways. On their hands they will bear you up, lest you strike your foot against a stone" (Ps. 91:11–12). We associate this psalm with the Messiah because Satan quotes it to Jesus during the wilderness temptation. But the word messiah doesn't appear in the psalm.

The writer of Hebrews echoes this thought. Of angels he wrote, "Are they not all ministering spirits sent out to serve for the sake of those who are to inherit salvation?" (Heb. 1:14). This verse strongly suggests that each believer has an unseen assistant through life.

The Bible is filled with examples where angels are sent to protect believers when such protection is part of God's will. Angels protected and defended Lot (Gen. 19:16). They delivered Daniel (Dan. 6:22) and his three friends (Shadrach, Meshach, Abednego) from certain death (Dan. 3:24–28). Angels delivered Peter (Acts 12:6–11) from prison and comforted Paul when his life was in danger on his journey to Rome (Acts 27:21–26).

There is no theological or logical reason to presume, in defiance of these examples, that spirit guardians have not and will not be present in our lives. Hebrews 13:2 makes it clear that in many cases we may already have encountered them without ever knowing it: "Do not neglect to show hospitality to strangers, for thereby some have entertained angels unawares."

PART 3

THE CHURCH

CHAPTER 21

John 6 Is Not about the Lord's Supper

The observance of the Lord's Supper (i.e., Communion) is one of the more controversial doctrines between Christian denominations. It seems simple enough. Paul clearly connected the celebration with Jesus's last Passover (i.e., the Last Supper) when he wrote that Jesus "on the night when he was betrayed took bread, and when he had given thanks, he broke it, and said, 'This is my body which is for you. Do this in remembrance of me'" (1 Cor. 11:23–24). What could be controversial about that?

There are several points of disagreement over the Lord's Supper among Christians. For example, Christian traditions disagree on whether the elements (i.e., the bread and wine) *are* the actual body and blood of Jesus, *contain* the body and blood of Christ, if the body and blood are *spiritually present* in the elements, or whether the bread and wine merely *represent* the body and blood. This question in turn leads to another: Does partaking of the bread and wine accomplish anything spiritually in the partaker? That is, does the Lord's Supper convey grace to people, thereby bringing about some sort of spiritual growth or change in them? Typically, only the "representative view" (the belief that the bread and wine are merely symbolic of the body and blood of Jesus) denies that the ceremony conveys grace in some way to the partakers. The rest of the traditions that have the body and blood in some respect present in the bread and wine believe that partaking of those elements does *something* to the partaker.

Fundamentally, then, the way the doctrine of the Lord's Supper is embraced and taught goes back to the issue of whether the body and blood of Jesus are somehow present in the bread and wine. When one examines the accounts of the Last Supper in the Synoptic Gospels (Matt. 26:26–29; Mark 14:22–25; Luke 22:14–23) one discovers that there is no confusion about whether consuming the bread and wine means eating Jesus's flesh and drinking his blood. That misperception is found only in John 6:22–65, the lengthy scene where Jesus says, "I am the living bread that came down from heaven. If anyone eats of this bread, he will live forever. And the bread that I will give for the life of the world is my flesh.... Whoever feeds on my flesh and drinks my blood has eternal life" (John 6:51, 54).

Many have argued that Jesus later explains that he was referring to whether people believe in him or not (John 6:60–65), so John 6 cannot teach that the body and blood are actually present. But this misses a larger point: John's Gospel describes the Last Supper in John 13:21–30, not John 6. The bread of life scene is *not* connected to the event that Paul explicitly says in 1 Corinthians 11 is the basis for the Lord's Supper. This simple fact ought to influence how we understand the Lord's Supper.

CHAPTER 22

The Communion Table Isn't a Confessional Booth

The most extensive passage on the Lord's Supper in the New Testament comes in 1 Corinthians 11:17–34. Verses 27–29 have caused a good deal of discussion:

> Whoever, therefore, eats the bread or drinks the cup of the Lord in an unworthy manner will be guilty concerning the body and blood of the Lord. Let a person examine himself, then, and so eat of the bread and drink of the cup. For anyone who eats and drinks without discerning the body eats and drinks judgment on himself.

I have been in many churches that take the wording of these verses to mean that believers are in physical (and perhaps mortal) danger if they partake of the Lord's Supper without first confessing known sin. The command for participants to examine themselves and the potential to partake "in an unworthy manner" are the foundation for this interpretation.

This interpretation fails to consider the context of the whole passage. Paul is very clear (vv. 20–22) on what prompted his theological lesson about the Lord's Supper:

> When you come together, it is not the Lord's supper that you eat. For in eating, each one goes ahead with his own meal. One goes hungry, another gets drunk. What! Do you not have houses to eat and drink in? Or do you despise the church of God and humiliate those who have nothing?

This accusation seems odd until we realize that in the early church (just as at Passover and the original Last Supper) there was a *meal* associated with the Lord's Supper. We know from ancient descriptions of what the early Christians did that a "love feast" was tied to the observance of the Lord's Supper. Paul describes how the Corinthians were abusing the situation. Poor believers were not being adequately fed (or impeded in some way), while others were becoming gluttonous and drunk.

Paul then explained that the occasion wasn't a social gathering but a memorial service focused on Jesus (vv. 23–26). It is then that he warns about partaking "unworthily" (v. 27). The context tells us what he means: don't be a glutton, don't get drunk, and make sure the poor believers get enough. Believers needed to examine whether they were guilty of these abuses. Paul wasn't turning the celebration into a time of general confession of sin.

This interpretation is clear from Paul's concluding remarks: "So then, my brothers, when you come together to eat, wait for one another—if anyone is hungry, let him eat at home—so that when you come together it will not be for judgment" (vv. 33–34).

CHAPTER 23

What Was Paul Thinking When He Compared Baptism and Circumcision?

Few biblical doctrines have divided Christianity more than baptism. It seems that there are as many views of it as denominations. Various denominations disagree on its meaning and relationship to grace and faith—namely, what, if anything, does baptism accomplish in the heart and life of the one baptized? Others, such as Baptists, recognize immersion as the only legitimate *mode* of baptism (i.e., how it's done). Others sprinkle or pour water on the recipient. Do Christians agree on anything when it comes to baptism? Well, sort of.

All Christian groups agree that baptism has some relationship to circumcision, though what exactly that might be is another area of debate. The agreement comes from the inescapable fact that Paul compares the two in Colossians 2:11–12:

> In him also you were circumcised with a circumcision made without hands, by putting off the body of the flesh, by the circumcision of Christ, having been buried with him in baptism, in which you were also raised with him through faith in the powerful working of God, who raised him from the dead.

What's clear is that Paul associated one practice with the other. So he considered the two to be analogous in some way, but what was he thinking?

The best way to approach this question is to frame it by what we know. Paul taught that salvation was by grace through faith, not by good works or merit. We also know that Israelites were elect, but that election did not result in salvation. The sign of the covenant between God and elect Israel was circumcision (Gen. 17:9–14). These three thoughts now help us articulate an analogous relationship between circumcision and baptism. In short, *what we say about baptism needs to align with what was true about circumcision.*

What this means is that we allow Scripture to interpret Scripture. Did circumcision result in salvation for an Israelite? No. Many circumcised Israelites apostatized and worshipped other gods. Their membership in Israel, the elect nation, did not guarantee their salvation. There is no way an Israelite could worship Baal and be in right relationship to the God of the Bible. That means that baptism cannot result in salvation either. Circumcision could also not accomplish other things. It did not move the recipient to be closer to God. It did not produce believing faith. It had nothing to do with salvation, saving grace, or saving faith.

So what did circumcision do? It made the recipient a member of the elect community where the truth about the true God was taught. Hopefully, one day the recipient would embrace that truth in faith. Though Israelite women were by default members of the elect community, circumcision was also a theological message to them. In sum, *circumcision meant access to truth.* That's what baptism means, too, when it's applied to children or infants. This also is true of adults, though adult circumcision could also demonstrate that belief in the truth was already present. And so it is with adult baptism being a sign of faith in the gospel.

CHAPTER 24

Motion or Meaning—What's More Important for Baptism?

Previously we talked about the divergent views of the meaning and significance of baptism. Christians also disagree on the *mode* of baptism, that is, how it should be done. Some believe immersion is the proper mode. Others say it's sprinkling or pouring. Still others say it doesn't matter. How did it come to this?

Any discussion of the mode of baptism invariably turns to the Greek word translated "baptize" in the New Testament, *baptizō*. The word is closely related to another term, *baptō*. *Baptō* occurs four times in the New Testament, never in the context of water baptism (Luke 16:24; John 13:26 [2x]; Rev. 19:13), and means "to dip." The word *baptizō* then, it is argued, means the same thing. Romans 6:4–5, a passage that uses *baptizō*, is offered as a vivid illustration of dipping: "We were buried therefore with him by baptism into death, in order that, just as Christ was raised from the dead by the glory of the Father, we too might walk in newness of life." Death, burial, and resurrection depict the up and down movement of dipping. This is the gist of the argument for those who favor immersion.

Proponents of other modes argue (correctly) that the Septuagint, the Greek translation of the Old Testament used by the early church, uses *baptizō* to describe activities besides dipping and where dipping makes no sense. For example, Isaiah 24:1 describes being "overwhelmed" (*baptizō*) by lawlessness. The book of Sirach, a work not found in the Protestant Bible but which is included in the Septuagint, uses *baptizō* to describe the Old Testament *washing* requirement for someone who touched a corpse (Sirach 24:25). Even in the New Testament there is ambiguity to *baptizō*. In Luke 11:38 we learn that a Pharisee was surprised when he noticed that Jesus did not wash (*baptizō*) before a meal. Are we really to expect that the Pharisee expected Jesus to plunge himself under water before eating? Mark 7:3–4 is especially telling in this regard. Notice the two Greek terms used to describe the same act: "For the Pharisees and all the Jews do not eat unless they wash [*niptō*] their hands properly, holding to the tradition of the elders, and when they come from the marketplace, they do not eat unless they wash [*baptize*]."

In many ways, the key passage is Romans 6:4–5, quoted above. Those who prefer immersion emphasize the *motion* of death, burial, and resurrection. The movement or motion persuades them of immersion. But what if the meaning—and not the motion—of the death, burial, and resurrection is instead emphasized? I wrote earlier that the point of baptism was (ideally) an expression of faith in the gospel for adults, and (ideally) the inclusion of children in a community where the truth of the gospel is taught. Would not the meaning of the death, burial, and resurrection of Jesus in Romans 6:4–5 speak to both situations? For the adult, baptism by any mode could signify that he or she has embraced the gospel. And for parents who have their children baptized by any mode, they tell the world that their child will be part of a church where the truth of the gospel is preached so that someday they might believe?

If we are clear on what baptism does *not* do to the recipient, then the mode really comes down to this: What's more significant, the motion or the meaning?

CHAPTER 25

Let's Not Confuse the Eternal State with the Canon

Spiritual gifts are controversial, to say the least. But like every other doctrine, they have a context. And that context isn't divorced from three-quarters of the Bible, the Old Testament. As a young Christian teenager, I was taught that the sign gifts—things like healing or speaking in tongues—were not for today. That belief was based in part on 1 Corinthians 13:8–10:

> Love never ends. As for prophecies, they will pass away; as for tongues, they will cease; as for knowledge, it will pass away. For we know in part and we prophesy in part, but when the perfect comes, the partial will pass away.

The key thought here is "when the perfect comes, the partial will pass away." The "perfect," I was told, was the Bible. According to this view, now that we have the full revelation of God in the Bible, we don't need to speak in tongues, and it wouldn't make sense for God to give people prophetic visions.

My thinking on gifts has evolved a bit. Though I still think the great majority of claims to miraculous gifts are bogus, I think we need to let God be God. If he wants to empower someone—in line with the original Old Testament context and New Testament practice—he's free to do it.

As a biblical scholar, I can make a case for that approach. One thing I can't make a case for is what I was taught as a teenager. The "perfect" of 1 Corinthians 13:10 has nothing to do with the formation of the canon. That interpretation has a fatal flaw: it ignores the two verses that follow. Here's the verse in context:

> When the perfect comes, the partial will pass away. When I was a child, I spoke like a child, I thought like a child, I reasoned like a child. When I became a man, I gave up childish ways. For now we see in a mirror dimly, but then face to face. Now I know in part; then I shall know fully, even as I have been fully known.

Verse twelve very clearly isn't talking about the day we get our Bible. It's *eschatological* in outlook. Paul is contrasting our present experience with the one to come. The "perfect" is theological shorthand for the day when believers will experience the intimate presence of God, the day we all reach glory. The metaphor of the mirror is important. In ancient times, people didn't have the glass mirrors we do now. Their mirrors were metal, polished to the point where one could see their reflection but not in precise details with high definition. Our present experience of the Lord is like that. We have a glimpse. But someday, our encounter will be face to face, with nothing hidden or obscured.

CHAPTER 26

Sacraments or Ordinances—a Distinction Without a Difference?

Earlier we discussed the doctrines of baptism and the Lord's Supper (communion). Depending on the church or tradition, these two rites are referred to either as sacraments or ordinances. The word choice does in fact mean something.

In briefest terms, a sacrament is a religious ritual that is either a *means* or *sign* of grace. "Means" and "sign" are important qualifiers. Traditions that are "sacramental" see baptism and communion as either conferring saving grace or as a sign of saving grace in the life of the partaker. Traditions that prefer the term "ordinance" seek to firmly distinguish baptism and communion from saving grace. For "ordinance" traditions, both rituals are to be understood more as acts of obedience rather than something done as a means or sign of grace.

Much of sacramental thinking with respect to baptism stems from a failure to observe consistency between baptism and circumcision, two items Paul clearly connects in Colossians 2:10–12. Circumcision didn't confer grace to any Israelite. It didn't remove original sin. It didn't kickstart saving faith in the recipient. There is no text in the Bible that puts forth these ideas. Circumcised Israelites regularly became apostate, and so Paul's link between circumcision and baptism didn't have those ideas in view. Yet Catholicism teaches that baptism removes original sin. Some Protestant churches see it as implanting the seed of faith, linking it to election. But circumcision didn't guarantee the recipient would follow the Lord. Election and salvation were not synonyms in Israel, so it's poor theology to presume baptism, analogous to circumcision according to Paul, produces an outcome circumcision could not.

Failure to observe that John 6 was *not* part of the Last Supper or the Lord's Supper also contributes to sacramental confusion. The only way to have Jesus "present" in the elements is to view them as *being* his body and blood. Catholicism has the wine and bread "transubstantiated" into the literal body and blood and, consequently, ingested by the partaker. This is a literalization of John 6, a passage that *isn't* John's account of the Last Supper. Protestant denominations linked John 6 to communion as well but didn't want to be Catholic. The presumed solutions were that the Lord was present in/by/with/near/over/under the elements (noting Luther's famous agglomeration of descriptive prepositions) or present in some special way to assist the believer (i.e., conferring nonsaving grace) in Christian perseverance.

It is simpler—and more biblical—to view baptism and communion in light of their Old Testament connections: circumcision and Passover (1 Cor. 10:14–22). Neither conferred saving grace. Circumcision meant membership in a community where the truth about the true God was taught. It marked a promise kept by the true God to save a remnant of humanity. Passover commemorated that the salvation of that remnant was through faith in the true God. When Israelites believed that God would save them from the last fatal judgment on Egypt, the Lord passed over them. Neither circumcision nor Passover was about earning God's favor or achieving an outcome through a ritual.

CHAPTER 27

Are Spiritual Gifts Natural Abilities or Divine Dispensations?

The New Testament links the presence of the Holy Spirit—something shared by all believers—with gifting for service. We all want to know we have a role to play, so spiritual gifts generate interest. A related question is whether "gifting" means that believers are given abilities by the Spirit at their conversion or that the Spirit heightens natural abilities in the believer.

The New Testament discussion of spiritual gifts is surprisingly brief. The Greek word behind the concept of "spiritual gift," *charisma*, occurs only seventeen times, and all but one of those is in the writings of Paul (1 Peter 4:10). Paul writes in 1 Corinthians 12:4–11:

> Now there are varieties of gifts, but the same Spirit; and there are varieties of service, but the same Lord; and there are varieties of activities, but it is the same God who empowers them all in everyone. To each is given the manifestation of the Spirit for the common good. For to one is given through the Spirit the utterance of wisdom, and to another the utterance of knowledge according to the same Spirit, to another faith by the same Spirit, to another gifts of healing by the one Spirit, to another the working of miracles, to another prophecy, to

> another the ability to distinguish between spirits, to another various kinds of tongues, to another the interpretation of tongues. All these are empowered by one and the same Spirit, who apportions to each one individually as he wills.

Notice that all three persons of the Trinity are involved in this gifting. It would appear from this passage that each *charisma* ("spiritual gift") is dispensed to the believer. There is no evidence in the New Testament that believers had such gifts prior to conversion. Consequently, it seems that gifting at conversion is in view. However, some of the less spectacular gifts in this passage (e.g., wisdom) don't seem to need special dispensation.

Ephesians 4 also comments on the gifts given to the church by the Lord. Paul writes that when Christ ascended, "he gave gifts to men. . . . apostles, the prophets, the evangelists, the shepherds and teachers, to equip the saints for the work of ministry, for building up the body of Christ" (Eph. 4:8, 11–12). Each of these ministries requires certain skills. For example, Paul told Timothy to look for leaders who were *able* to teach (1 Tim. 3:2) and to challenge teachers to handle Scripture correctly (2 Tim. 2:15). If this were a supernaturally given ability, those exhortations seem odd. Instead, perhaps the Spirit of God provides the church with gifted people *providentially*, as opposed to supernaturally changing them at conversion.

Or perhaps the best answer is *both* are true. There's no scriptural reason why it must be one or the other. God can do as he wishes. If we're willing servants, he'll put us where he wants us and make us fit for the task.

CHAPTER 28

When the Twelve Apostles Died, Apostolic Authority Died with Them

Some denominations hold to apostolic succession, which is the notion that church authority can be traced to the original apostles through transmission by practices like the laying on of hands or ordination. This reflects a misunderstanding of the term "apostle" in the New Testament.

The word "apostle" occurs nearly eighty times in the New Testament. In the Gospels and most instances in the book of Acts, the term refers to the original men who were called by Jesus to be his followers. The original apostles were known collectively as the Twelve (John 6:67; 20:24) or the eleven after Judas forsook the calling (Acts 1:25–26).

It was the Twelve in whom authority in the fledgling church rested. Why? These men had been taught personally by Jesus during his earthly ministry. The experience of being personally discipled by the incarnate Christ was what gave them their authority. The case of Matthias, the man chosen by lot to replace Judas, was something of an exception (Acts 1:26). Interestingly, Acts 1:21 indicates that the criteria for being considered a replacement was *still* earthly contact with Jesus *before* his death and resurrection. Only "men who have accompanied us during all the time that the Lord Jesus went in and out among us" were acceptable. Of the two who met the criteria,

Matthias was chosen. Paul was an apostle, but (obviously) not one of the Twelve. The fact that Paul's apostleship was repeatedly questioned stems from this circumstance. It is telling that, on the occasions when Paul defended his apostleship, Paul points to the fact that he was indeed personally called by Jesus (Acts 9) and given his doctrine by direct revelation from the resurrected Christ (Gal. 1:11–12), apparently over the course of three years (Gal. 1:16–18). That contact put him on the same level as the original apostles and Matthias for approximately the same duration.

The laying on of hands was part of publicly approving and identifying with the servant leadership of the church (deacons, elders), but these leaders were not called apostles in the New Testament. There is no single verse in the New Testament where "apostle" and "elder" even appear together. When "apostles" and "elders" are mentioned in proximity (e.g., Acts 15:2, 4, 6, 22, 23; 16:4) the groups are distinct. The apostles in such cases were the surviving members of the original twelve disciples and Matthias, who joined the original eleven after being chosen by lot to replace Judas (Acts 1:26). "Elders" was a traditional term used for the leadership of the communal people of God all the way back into the Old Testament (e.g., Ex. 18). Those few occasions where "apostle" is used of people other than the Twelve or Paul in the letters of the New Testament refer in context to people "sent" (the meaning of "apostle" is "sent one") to minister to various churches. The term is typically translated "messenger" in those cases (Phil. 2:25; 2 Cor. 8:23) and is akin to the way we describe missionaries. None of these circumstances give them an equal status to the original Twelve. And contemporary church leaders don't have that status either.

CHAPTER 29

The Baptism of the Holy Spirit Isn't about Speaking in Tongues

I note earlier that spiritual gifts are controversial. Part of the confusion over how to process them is the matter of the baptism of the Holy Spirit. Rather than rely on popular tradition, we need to let the New Testament be our guide on this topic. It's actually pretty clear what this baptism is—and isn't.

The idea of Spirit baptism surfaces in the Gospels (Matt. 3:11; Mark 1:8; Luke 3:16). Just before the resurrected Jesus ascended to heaven, he told his followers to wait for this Spirit baptism, promising it would come "not many days from now" (Acts 1:5). Sure enough, shortly thereafter, the Spirit came in force on the day of Pentecost (Acts 2:1–13). On that occasion, the followers of Jesus were enabled to speak with other tongues (known languages) to preach the gospel to Jews from all over the known world who'd come to Jerusalem for Pentecost. Why? So that they could return to the nations where they'd been scattered centuries earlier. They would infiltrate the nations and bring the gospel to other Jews and gentiles. Pentecost launched the reclaiming of the nations disinherited by God at Babel.

The logic of the baptism of the Spirit is crucial for understanding the concept. Spirit baptism was connected to the evangelization of Jews and gentiles, beginning in Jerusalem and spreading out to the whole world. Throughout the book of Acts, the disciples ran into unexpected conversions. They at first assumed the gospel was only for Israelites (Jews), since the Messiah was the son of David. But soon the message of Jesus had been embraced by proselytes (converts to Judaism by non-Jews; Acts 6:5; 13:43), Jews who identified with gentile (Greek) culture ("Hellenists"; Acts 6:1), half-breed Jews (Samaritans; Acts 8:4–8), and, most shockingly, pagan gentiles (Acts 10). The validation that these conversions were real was the reception of the Holy Spirit (Acts 10:44–47; 15:8). The disciples even made journeys to lay hands on converts to give them the Holy Spirit (Acts 8:15–17). They assumed that the Spirit would join them to the company of believers or reject them.

It's important to point out that there is no mention of tongues in all these non-Jewish receptions of the Spirit. The initial kick-starting of the church, who were a "circumcision neutral" people of God, included miraculous gifting to speak in other languages. That was actually a fulfillment of Old Testament prophecy (Isa. 28:11–12; cf. 1 Cor. 14:21). Spirit baptism (or reception) in Acts wasn't focused on tongues. Rather, its purpose was to telegraph something new: God was forming one family whose membership included *anyone* who embraced the gospel of Jesus, Jew or otherwise. Paul was clear on this point: "For in one Spirit we were all baptized into one body—Jews or Greeks, slaves or free—and all were made to drink of one Spirit" (1 Cor. 12:13).

PART 4

ISRAEL

CHAPTER 30

The Historic Covenants God Made with Israel Were Conditionally Unconditional

A covenant is an agreement, akin to a contractual relationship in our culture. Most of the Old Testament unfolds in the context of the covenant relationships God initiated with Israel during the days of Abraham, Moses, and David. These covenants do not merely form a framework for the biblical history of Israel. They propel core ideas in biblical theology that are essential for understanding the message of the Bible.

It is common for students of Scripture to assume that these covenants had nothing to do with the performance of Israelites because God initiated the covenant relationships with his people. God is a forgiving God, so the reasoning goes, and therefore the promises given in the covenants would never be nullified. This reasoning isn't quite consistent with what we see in Scripture when we examine the covenants closely. They are both conditional and unconditional.

When God made a covenant with Abraham, he promised that Abraham's descendants would be multiplied, settle in a land of their own, and would be a blessing to the other nations (Gen. 12:1–3). The plan was unconditional. The behavior of Abraham's offspring (the Israelites) would not overturn God's plan. But whether individual

Israelites enjoyed the blessings of the covenant depended on the condition of their faithfulness. Abraham had to obey God (Gen. 17:1–2, 8–10; 22:15–18); he could not arbitrarily decide to reject circumcision or follow another god.

The same was true for his descendants. The events at Sinai and the subsequent wilderness wanderings on the way to the promised land made that painfully clear. Not only did God's law instruct Israel on how to be faithful worshippers of God, but the promise of occupying the land was specifically linked to loyalty to Yahweh and his law (Lev. 26; Deut. 4:25–27, 39–40; 11:18–24). Leviticus 26 and Deuteronomy 27–29 lay out in unmistakable detail how Israel will be cursed and driven into exile should they be unfaithful to God. And that's just what happened.

The covenant with David (2 Sam. 7) worked the same way. God promised David that only men from his dynasty would legitimately occupy the throne of Israel. In Psalm 89:20–37 God vowed that he wouldn't turn his back on his promise even if David's descendants forsook his law, but he added in the same passage that those who sinned would be punished for unfaithfulness. God could and did remove unfaithful kings, even those from David's line.

All this plays out in the New Testament in two ways. A perfect descendant of David who was always faithful to God's law would fulfill the covenants. His name was Jesus. And through Jesus, a new people of God, the church, would benefit from the covenant promises. As we'll see later, this affects other areas of theology.

CHAPTER 31

The Tower of Babel Is the Backdrop for the Old Testament Theology of Election

Typically when we think of election, we think of two things: (1) the nation of Israel and (2) that election speaks of salvation. The latter is a demonstrably flawed idea. The former is more in the ballpark, since election was really about access to the true God, which was something only Israel had. But how did Israel get in that position?

The backdrop for Israel's elect status is the tower of Babel story (Gen. 11:1–9). But you won't understand what I mean by reading Genesis. Instead, we need to turn to another passage that references the division of the nations, the judgment of Babel in Deuteronomy 32:8–9:

> When the Most High apportioned the nations
> as an inheritance,
> when he divided up humankind,
> he established the borders of the peoples
> according to the number of the sons of God.
> But the LORD's portion is his people,
> Jacob his allotted heritage.

When God divided the nations by confusing their languages, he distributed the nations among "the sons of God," which can refer to angels or in this case demons.

Think about what all this means. Prior to this point in biblical history, God had a relationship with all humanity. The disobedience after the flood showed that the flood hadn't cured the propensity of the hearts of people to wander from God. He'd had enough. At Babel God disinherited humanity, the nations, from being his children. And that set the stage for what happened in the biblical drama next.

Right after the judgment at Babel God called Abraham (Gen. 12), he *chose* one man and his wife, who were past the point of childbearing, to raise up a new family for himself. *That* is how Israel came to be the people of the true, incomparable God. *That* is why Israel was *elect*. It's also why the rest of the Old Testament story is "Yahweh vs. the gods" and "Israel vs. the nations." Whether we realize it or not, this worldview doesn't go away in the New Testament. It's just as real there, which has staggering theological implications.

CHAPTER 32

The Church Is a New Israel

The Bible is obviously divided into the Old and New Testaments. This division is so obvious to any student of Scripture that it's sometimes difficult to see the connections between the two. An important case in point is the relationship between Israel and the church.

Many Christians steadfastly resist seeing continuity between Israel and the church as one people of God, preferring instead to speak of two completely distinct peoples of God, Israel and the church. The reason for the wall of separation between them is that certain beliefs about end times seem impossible or unlikely without such a separation. But it's never wise to throw the baby out with the bath water, even in theology. The New Testament is crystal clear that, in some sense, the church is a new Israel.

Paul states this theological reality explicitly in several places. His most forceful statement of it comes in Galatians 3:

> And the Scripture, foreseeing that God would justify the Gentiles by faith, preached the gospel beforehand to Abraham, saying, "In you shall all the nations be blessed." . . . so that in Christ Jesus the blessing of Abraham might come to the Gentiles, so that we might receive the promised Spirit through faith. . . . for in Christ Jesus you are all sons of God, through faith. For as many of you as were baptized into Christ

> have put on Christ. There is neither Jew nor Greek, there is neither slave nor free, there is no male and female, for you are all one in Christ Jesus. And if you are Christ's, then you are Abraham's offspring, heirs according to promise. (Gal. 3:8, 14, 26–28)

In this passage, Paul—a Jew, the physical descendant of Abraham—says point-blank that gentiles are also Abraham's offspring and have inherited the covenantal promise given to Abraham's children, namely, Israel. As Paul says elsewhere, it may be a "mystery," but it's true that "the Gentiles are fellow heirs, members of the same body, and partakers of the promise in Christ Jesus through the gospel" (Eph. 3:6).

It's easy to understand, then, why Paul proclaims, "Not all who are descended from Israel belong to Israel, and not all are children of Abraham because they are his offspring" (Rom. 9:6–7). All who embrace the gospel are united into one "circumcision neutral" people of God, the body of Christ, the church, whether they are Abraham's physical offspring (Israel) or not (gentiles). Paul makes this point unmistakable in Galatians 6:15–16 when he says to gentile listeners, "For neither circumcision counts for anything, nor uncircumcision, but a new creation. And as for all who walk by this rule, peace and mercy be upon them, and upon the Israel of God."

CHAPTER 33

The Promised Land: Forfeited, Fulfilled, or yet Future?

As we saw earlier, the New Testament explicitly affirms the church, who are the "circumcision neutral" people of God, to be a new Israel having inherited the promises given to Abraham (Gal. 3:26–29). Yet despite the clarity of what Paul says in Galatians, the passage curiously omits reference to the land element of the promises to Abraham—specifically, the promise that the land of Canaan was to be the possession of Abraham's descendants (Gen. 12:1; 15:7). Why the silence? There are several possible explanations.

Many Christians understand the silence of Paul to indicate that the land promises given to Abraham and his offspring, the Israelites, are still in effect. The implication of such a view is that the physical descendants of Abraham, defined today as anyone claiming the ethnic identify of "Jew," have a God-given claim to the land known today as Israel. It is further asserted that this promise will only be fulfilled when the Lord returns to rule in that land. The present reality of the land promise, then, is seen to be central to the doctrine of the future millennial kingdom (Rev. 20:1–6).

Other Christians disagree. Some argue that Paul's silence is due to Israel's forfeiture of the promise. The Old Testament is quite clear that possession of the promised land was conditioned on faithfulness to God (Deut. 4:25–27, 39–40; 11:18–24; Lev. 26).

Since Israel forsook the Lord and was subsequently sent into exile, the land element of the promise was lost by Israel because of her sin.

Still other Christians prefer a third perspective. They point out that certain passages that detail the dimensions of the promised land (Gen. 15:18; Ex. 23:31) align very closely to the borders of the kingdom under Solomon, the son of David (1 Kings 4:21). This would seemingly indicate that the land promised to Abraham was indeed fully inherited. Paul is silent in Galatians 3 because the promise has already been fulfilled, so there's no need to bring it up.

Lastly, some presume that since Galatians 3 (and other passages) expand the people of God to include all the nations (gentiles), the land element of the original promise extends to the lands of those nations. Paul's silence would therefore indicate that the "promised land" is now the whole world—every nation without exception. This view points to the global Edenic kingdom in Revelation 21–22 as validation of this idea.

So who is right? We don't know, and we honestly can't with certainty. Believing scholars have adopted each view since Scripture itself doesn't provide precise clarity. The lesson, then, is not to pretend that whatever view we prefer is the self-evident "biblical" one. It's presumptuous to assert more certainty than Scripture offers.

CHAPTER 34

Israelite Circumcision Had Theological Meaning for Women

The story of Abraham and Sarah is at the core of the story of Israel. God called Abraham (Gen. 12:1–3; 15:1–6) and told him that he would make his offspring like the sand of the sea and the stars of the sky. There was just one problem. Abraham and his wife were old.

Sarah, in fact, was well past child-bearing years and for many years after God's initial promise, could not conceive a child (Gen. 16:1–6; Heb. 11:11). Her inability to conceive led to Sarah's proposal that Abraham have children with her handmaiden, Hagar. The result was the birth of Ishmael, whom God told Abraham in no uncertain terms was *not* the fulfillment of his original promise (Gen. 17:15–21; Heb. 11:17–18). He would enable Sarah to have a child.

God was of course true to his promise. Abraham and Sarah had Isaac. When God corrected Abraham about Ishmael and clarified that Sarah herself would indeed have the promised child, God initiated a sign to commemorate the covenant promise: circumcision (Gen. 17:1–14).

The sign of the covenant meant that every male in Abraham's household had to be circumcised. The requirement extended to all males born to every family in the nation of Israel because all Israelites were descendants of Abraham through Isaac.

Circumcision seems like an odd sign, not only because of the physical nature of the mark, but also because it seems so one-sided. What possible relevance could circumcision have for Israelite women?

Because of the sexual nature of the sign of circumcision, the ritual mark was an important theological reminder to both genders. The sign would have taken the mind of both men and women back to the fact that they and their children only existed because of divine intervention.

Women would also have been reminded of the importance of having husbands who were members of the Israelite community in order to pass on the bloodline of Abraham, Isaac, and Jacob. Bearing children to gentile men in Old Testament times would have been a covenant transgression unless the man joined the people of Israel (which required circumcision).

As unusual as the sign seems to us today, it was a theological statement in its time. This highlights one of the important tasks of rituals—to draw attention to a transcendent idea.

CHAPTER 35

Israelites Were Forgiven through Animal Sacrifice in the Old Testament, but Those Sacrifices Did Not Atone for Many Kinds of Sin

For most lay Bible students, much of the Old Testament is a mystery. That shouldn't be a surprise since the culture of the ancient Near Eastern world is so foreign, and because most preachers confine their Old Testament preaching to Genesis, Exodus, and character sketches of Old Testament figures. This is unfortunate, since the Old Testament was the Bible of Jesus and the apostles. Old Testament theology is the beginning point for understanding the theology of three-quarters of your Bible *as well as* being the frame of reference for New Testament theology.

One of the most significant gaps in Christian knowledge of the Old Testament is the sacrificial system. It's easy to read statements in the book of Hebrews about how the sacrifice of Jesus was superior (e.g., Heb. 10:1–18) and conclude that Old Testament sacrifices accomplished nothing other than producing dead carcasses. That isn't what the Old Testament says.

The book of Leviticus lays out the sacrificial system of ancient Israel. It says repeatedly that the sacrifices resulted in forgiveness for the one who brought the sacrifice. Leviticus 4:20 is representative:

"Thus shall he do with the bull. As he did with the bull of the sin offering, so shall he do with this. And the priest shall make atonement for them, and they shall be forgiven" (cf. Lev. 4:26, 31, 35; 5:10, 13, 16, 18). But if Old Testament sacrifices resulted in forgiveness, how does the writer of Hebrews say, "It is impossible for the blood of bulls and goats to take away sins" (Heb. 10:4)?

That's the verse about sacrifices that many Christians seem to know. But they miss this one: "Under the law almost everything is purified with blood, and *without* the shedding of blood there is no forgiveness of sins" (Heb. 9:22). The verse clearly has blood sacrifice as necessary for forgiveness. Thus Hebrews is consistent with Leviticus. But again, what's up with Hebrews 10:4?

First, it's important to realize that the goal of sacrifice was to restore ritual purity (access to sacred areas), not to atone for moral offenses. Israelites might become impure and disqualified to enter sacred space for all sorts of reasons, including but not limited to acts of sin. Second, there were many sins for which sacrifice had no value at all. Capital offenses required the death penalty. Crimes against other people were dealt with by restorative punishments (see Ex. 21–23). Deliberate ("high-handed" or presumptive) sins against God could not be atoned for by sacrifice (Num. 15:30–31).

Christ's cross bridges these (and other) gaps. Permanent reconciliation to God for any sin could be obtained only through the sacrifice of Jesus on the cross. That's why the sacrifice of Jesus was superior.

PART 5

GOD: FATHER, SON, AND SPIRIT

CHAPTER 36

The Presence of the Holy Spirit with Believers in the Old Testament Was Occasional and Temporary

We tend to think about the Holy Spirit with New Testament blinders on. There are plenty of passages in the New Testament affirming that the Spirit of God indwells every believer (John 7:37–39; Acts 11:16–17; Rom. 5:5; 8:9–11; 1 Cor. 2:12; 2 Cor. 5:5). Every believer is "sealed with the promised Holy Spirit, who is the guarantee of our inheritance until we acquire possession of it, to the praise of his glory" (Eph. 1:13–14).

If this is what we're thinking about the Holy Spirit, it's no surprise that what goes on in the Old Testament raises questions. I've met many believers who seem convinced that passages like Psalm 51:11, written in the wake of David's sin with Bathsheba, is proof that we can sin away our salvation (see the psalm's *superscription*; cf. 2 Samuel 11). That understanding of Psalm 51:11 is flawed. It fails to consider the ministry of the Spirit as it's described in the Old Testament.

In the Old Testament, the language that describes the Holy Spirit's relationship to people varies, yet it consistently shows the Spirit coming upon people to enable them for a specific task. For example, the Spirit enabled Joseph (Gen. 41:38) and Daniel (Dan. 4:8; 5:11–14; 6:3) to interpret dreams. On several occasions, the

Spirit "came upon" prophets (Num. 24:2; 1 Sam. 10:6, 10; 2 Chron. 15:1) and judges (Judg. 3:10; 6:34; 11:29; 13:25) to empower them. Artisans were "filled" with the Spirit for the work on the tabernacle (Ex. 31:3; 35:31). And prophets had visions after being "lifted" by the Spirit (Ezek. 3:12; 8:3; 11:1, 24).

One of the most important enabling acts of the Spirit concerned the Israelite king. The presence of the Spirit came upon David as soon as he was anointed king: "Then Samuel took the horn of oil and anointed him in the midst of his brothers. And the Spirit of the LORD rushed upon David from that day forward" (1 Sam. 16:13).

The association of the Spirit with kings Saul (1 Sam. 10:6, 10) and David (1 Sam. 16:13) is the context for David's prayer in Psalm 51:11. If the Spirit of God left King David it would have been an indication that God was stripping him of the kingship, just as God did with King Saul (1 Sam. 16:14). In Psalm 51, David wasn't hoping he hadn't lost his salvation; he feared losing the kingship and the presence of God with it.

CHAPTER 37

Jesus Wasn't God's Only Son

With this chapter's title, I'm guessing I have your attention.

John 3:16 is like the song *Amazing Grace*—everyone has heard it at least once. In the old King James Version it went like this: "For God so loved the world, that he gave his only begotten Son, that whosoever believeth in him should not perish, but have everlasting life." Modern translations typically don't have "only begotten" in the verse but, oddly enough, you'll still find it in other verses in very recent translations. The ESV, for example, renders Hebrew 5:5 this way: "So also Christ did not exalt himself to be made a high priest, but was appointed by him who said to him, 'You are my Son, today I have begotten you.'"

The "only begotten" language is quaint. Even if Bible readers don't quite understand what it means, they sense it's supposed to mark Jesus as the only son of God. The problem is, that isn't biblically true.

Folks who have read the Bible closely know that God has other sons. There are heavenly "sons of God" in Scripture (e.g., Gen. 6:2, 4; Job 1:6; 2:1; 38:7). There are divine "sons of the Most High" (Ps. 82:6). God referred to the Israelites corporately as "my son" (Ex. 4:22; Hos. 11:1). The Israelite king was also the son of God (Ps. 2:7).

This is all well and good, but we know from a variety of passages that Jesus was in a league of his own. He was different than all other sons of God . . . wasn't he? He was, and the New Testament telegraphs that with a special term.

The Greek word behind the KJV's "only begotten" is *monogenēs*. In the late nineteenth century, many scholars presumed the word came from two other Greek words: *monos* ("only") and the verb *gennaō* ("to beget, give birth to"). Hence the antiquated translation "only begotten." Later discoveries, however, established that *monogenēs* has nothing to do with a beginning or point of origin. It actually comes from *monos* ("only") and the noun *genos* ("class, kind"). The term literally refers to something that is "one of a kind" or *unique*. We can know for certain this is what the term means because of Hebrews 11:17, where we are told that Abraham was ready to offer up his "only" (*monogenēs*) son (cf. Gen 22). But Isaac wasn't Abraham's only son. He wasn't even his first son (that was Ishmael; Gen. 16:11–15). But Isaac was in fact *unique*. He was the son of the promise, the one born through supernatural assistance (Gen. 18:9–15; 21:12).

The proper meaning of the term is actually important for understanding Jesus. God didn't have a beginning. But the incarnation marked something new. The eternal, unique Son would become a man in Jesus.

CHAPTER 38

The Firstborn of All Creation Didn't Have a Beginning

In his letter to the Colossians, Paul described Jesus in a way that has unnecessarily disquieted many Christians:

> He is the image of the invisible God, the firstborn of all creation. For by him all things were created, in heaven and on earth, visible and invisible, whether thrones or dominions or rulers or authorities—all things were created through him and for him. (Col. 1:15–16)

The cause for concern is that Jesus is called the *firstborn*. Many opponents of historic Christianity, which affirms a Trinity and requires Jesus to be God, have argued that a label like "firstborn" suggests that Jesus had a beginning. They're not worried about the birth of Jesus of Nazareth in this claim. They're worried that, long before Jesus was born to Mary, God created a divine figure (with a beginning) who appeared as Jesus of Nazareth. This figure, we are told, was God's agent of creation: God's first creation, who in turn created everything else. But this being, because he had a beginning, cannot be eternal. By definition, that means he cannot be God.

This understanding of "firstborn" might seem logical, but it has serious flaws. First, this understanding of Jesus as a created being must be divorced from other things Paul says about Jesus that affirm he was truly God. Incredibly, Philippians 2:6–11 informs us that Jesus did not think "equality" with God (v. 6) was something to be held onto instead of coming to earth to die for humanity. Instead, Jesus "emptied himself, by taking the form of a servant, being born in the likeness of men" (v. 7). Second, this view also ignores other New Testament passages that have Jesus as God, and thus preexistent. John 1:1–3 describes Jesus as the agent of creation in terms similar to Colossians 1:15–16. John asserts, "In the beginning was the Word, and the Word was with God, and the Word was God. He was in the beginning with God. All things were made through him, and without him was not any thing made that was made." John adds, "And the Word became flesh and dwelt among us" (John 1:14).

An equally serious flaw comes from the way Jews, such as Paul, would have understood the term "firstborn" in light of the Old Testament. In Psalm 89:27 God says he will make David "the firstborn, the highest of the kings of the earth." David was not his father's firstborn son. The kings of Israel were not required to be the firstborn sons of their fathers. Rather, "firstborn" refers to special status and rank. Since Jesus was in the line of David, which was a requirement for kingship, it makes sense to call him the "firstborn" in messianic contexts because of Psalm 89. This exalted status explains why God chose the Son to be the agent of creation. None of the other sons of God would do. They could only watch (Job 38:7–8) while the eternal Son went to work.

CHAPTER 39

The Holy Spirit Is Not an Impersonal Force

Other than "the third person of the Trinity," many Christians would find it difficult to describe the Holy Spirit. Because we live conscious lives in a body of flesh, the notion of a disembodied *person* is hard to fathom. It would be like "meeting" someone invisible—and who didn't speak either. Can a person be intangible and imperceptible?

Despite the fact that the idea is a bit incomprehensible to us, the Bible presents the Holy Spirit as a person in a number of ways. The most familiar is the way it aligns the Spirit with God and Jesus in what theologians call "Trinitarian formulas." The most well-known is probably Matthew 28:19: "Go therefore and make disciples of all nations, baptizing them in the name of the Father and of the Son and of the Holy Spirit" (cf. 1 Cor. 12:4–6; 2 Cor. 13:14). It would be very odd for biblical writers to do this if they did not view the Spirit as a person.

But that still doesn't help us describe the Holy Spirit. In my years of teaching the Bible, I've heard a few attempts to describe the Spirit like this one: "an energy field created by all living things that surrounds us, penetrates us, and binds everything together." That seems to fit, at least a little. God and the Holy Spirit are omnipresent, so it's fair to say that one, the other, or both could be simultaneously near and in everything and everyone. But science exposes a flaw in this definition. Energy is "the capacity of a physical system to perform work."* Energy is part of our material world, so the Holy Spirit cannot be energy if he is somehow inextricably linked to God and Jesus. It's just as well, since the description you read above is exactly how Obi-Wan Kenobi defined the force in *Star Wars*.

Not only is the Spirit connected to God and Jesus, but the Bible speaks of the Holy Spirit as an individual *person* like the Father and the Son. For example, the Spirit is characterized as a being who acts with intentionality, can communicate, who possesses and transmits knowledge, and who makes decisions (e.g., 1 Sam. 16:14; Ezek. 2:2; Acts 8:29; 10:19; 20:22; John 14:26; 1 Cor. 12:11). The Holy Spirit is also said to be affected by other persons, namely us. He can be grieved (Eph. 4:30), stifled (1 Thess. 5:19), and resisted (Acts 7:51). As with the Trinitarian formulas, speaking of the Spirit in such ways would be very peculiar for writers who did not consider the Spirit a person.

The takeaway for the believer is that if the Spirit is indeed a person, then by definition he takes a personal interest in us. He is not assigned to us by God the Father against his will. Rather, he is our personal helper, guide, and advocate (John 14:16–17, 26; 15:26; Rom. 8:26–27).

---

* Andrew Zimmerman Jones, "Energy: A Scientific Definition," ThoughtCo, August 10, 2017, http://physics.about.com/od/glossary/g/energy.htm

CHAPTER 40

God Came to People as a Man before Jesus

Most Christians are familiar with the story of how God visited Abraham (Gen. 12:1–9). The story opens with a command: "Now the LORD said to Abram, 'Go from your country and your kindred and your father's house to the land that I will show you'" (Gen. 12:1). God then proceeded to make certain promises to Abram (Abraham), that he and his wife Sarah would have a child, and from that child a nation would be born, live in the place God granted them, and be a blessing to all other nations.

But that isn't the whole story. Later in the same chapter we read: "Then the LORD appeared to Abram and said, 'To your offspring I will give this land.' So he built there an altar to the LORD, who had appeared to him" (Gen. 12:7). Twice we are told that God *appeared* to Abraham. This description goes beyond hearing a voice. Abraham saw God. Abraham saw God at other times, too. In Genesis 15 Abraham sees God in a vision (Gen. 15:1). In Genesis 18 God comes to Abraham with two angels (Gen. 18–19), and they share a meal (Gen. 18:1–8) and have an important conversation (Gen. 18:22–33; cf. Gen. 19:1). The other patriarchs saw God as well. The LORD appeared to Isaac (Gen. 26:1–5), the son God had promised Abraham, and Jacob, the son of Isaac (Gen. 28:10–22; 31:11–12; 32:24–30).

Genesis 12 and 15 both describe God appearing to Abraham to form a covenant relationship with him. Both have Abraham seeing God. But there's something in Genesis 15:1's appearance that is easily missed but very significant. It wasn't just God who appeared to Abraham. The text says, "The *word* of the LORD came to Abram in a vision." The "Word" was God, the very same description that John later applied to Jesus (John 1:1–3).

The word of the LORD makes other visible appearances in the Old Testament. One of my favorites is 1 Samuel 3. The boy Samuel kept hearing a voice calling his name while he was trying to sleep. This happened three times. Finally, in verse 10 we read: "Then the LORD came and *stood there* and called out as before, 'Samuel! Samuel!'" We know this was God in human form since the description has him standing, and since the end of the chapter (1 Sam. 3:19–20) says that "the word of the LORD" made a habit of appearing to Samuel.

Jeremiah too had the "word of the LORD" come to him in physical human form (Jer. 1:1–9). Jeremiah identified the speaker as the LORD himself, and the LORD touched Jeremiah *with his hand* (Jer. 1:9).

These incidents (and others) prepared God's people for the incarnation, when this same God would be born of Mary as Jesus of Nazareth.

CHAPTER 41

God Neither Causes nor Needs Evil

The relationship of God to evil and sin is a theological question that almost every Christian cares about. We believe, of course, that God exists and is sovereign. We know evil exists by virtue of our experience. Therein lies the conundrum. If God is in control of everything and evil exists, then it must exist because God either desires, permits, or needs its existence. The first option produces an evil, twisted deity. The second makes God a little less warped, but portrays him as apparently indifferent and insufficiently moved by our plight to eradicate the cause. The third prompts the question of how an omniscient God couldn't come up with a better plan.

All three formulations should be rejected. They are all propelled by some flawed thinking. First, the notion of God's sovereignty is too often defined as God predestinating everything. God's foreknowledge does not necessitate predestination. The fact that God knew evil would enter into the world (because he knows all things real and possible) doesn't require that he decreed the fall or any other evil thereafter. Second, we share God's attributes as his imagers. So do the members of his heavenly host. One of the attributes God shares with all his imagers is freedom. We are not robots with our acts predestined or programmed. If we were, we would not be like God, and we would not be his image.

These observations mean that evil exists because of God's decision to share his freedom with created beings who lack his perfectly holy character. The horrendous atrocities we hear about every day do not exist because God wanted his creatures to suffer. Evil is not part of life because God decided to weave it into his plan for the ages, as though it's necessary for everything to work out in the end. Evil doesn't exist because God just tolerates it either, as though he's unwilling to do something about it.

God's decision to make humans and the divine beings that serve him in his image—and therefore capable of making choices—also means that eliminating evil would require the extermination of all his imagers. God could do that. He is all-powerful. But God is also love (1 John 4:8). God knew what would result from his initial choice to make intelligent beings like himself. He knew rebellion and evil would come and what that would mean. But he deemed that consequence preferable to never having children, whether the "sons of God" or us.

Rather than destroy us all, God chose to forgive and redeem. Using his loyal and loving imagers, he guides the restoration of his good Edenic rule, his kingdom, forward through history toward its proper end. His wisdom and power transcend our choices. In the end, he will have his way without eliminating free will or those who exercise it.

CHAPTER 42

The Humanity of Jesus Is as Important as His Deity

What's the first answer that comes to mind when you hear the question, "Who is Jesus?" If you're a Christian, chances are high that your response would be something like "Jesus is God" or "Jesus is the savior of the world." Those are of course theologically on target. But they are illustrative of the way Christians emphasize the divine nature of Jesus and the supernatural effects of his work on the cross more than the fact that he was a man.

This fixation on the deity of Christ is no surprise. Belief in the Trinity requires it. There is no atonement or salvation without it. But the theological reality is that those doctrines would fade away just as quickly if the humanity of Jesus was compromised. This may seem like an odd assertion, but think about why Jesus had to be truly human.

After the fall, God warned the serpent that one of Eve's offspring would strike back against the ruin he had brought upon humanity (Gen. 3:15). The descendants of Eve could only be human. No mere mortal would be able to confront the devil and undo the harm he'd done, but the one who would do that had to be human.

When God made a covenant with Abraham, the patriarch was told that through his offspring all the nations that had been disinherited by God at Babel would one day be blessed—brought back to the true God (Gen. 12:3; 22:18). Paul tells us directly that Jesus was this promised offspring: "Now the promises were made to Abraham and to his offspring. It does not say, 'And to offsprings,' referring to many, but referring to one, 'And to your offspring,' who is Christ" (Gal. 3:16). Abraham's children were human, and so the one descendant who would fulfill the covenant with Abraham had to be human.

In 2 Samuel 7 God made a covenant with David. God promised that David's dynastic line would never end and that only David's sons would rightfully be Israel's kings (cf. Ps. 89:20–29). God went so far as to say that if David's sons forsook his law they would be punished, but he would not annul his covenant with David's line (Ps. 89:29–36). We know from Old Testament history that David's descendants did forsake God's law and worship other gods. The kingship of David's house was suspended, awaiting the day when a sinless son of David would arrive and take the throne. That son was Jesus (Rom. 1:3), and since David's children were necessarily human, Jesus had to be a man.

There are other reasons the humanity of Jesus is important, such as his ability to identify with our plight (Heb. 2:18; 4:15) and to play the role of a second, sinless Adam (Rom. 5). But the covenants that propel biblical theology are at the heart of why his humanity is essential.

CHAPTER 43

Jesus Is and Isn't God

One of the fundamental points of Christian theology is the deity of Jesus Christ—the belief that Jesus of Nazareth was truly the God of the Old Testament, born of a woman, living as a human being. But Christ's divinity does not mean that God was nowhere else when he lived on earth. Both God and Jesus simultaneously existed (as they had before Jesus was born). While on earth Jesus referred to God as "Father." Consequently, Trinitarianism speaks of "God the Father" and "God the Son" (Jesus). The third person of this Trinity is the Holy Spirit. So even though Jesus is God, he is not the Father—hence the play on words in this chapter's title: Jesus is God, but he isn't God (the Father).

Jesus is identified as God in several ways in the New Testament. Scripture describes him as having attributes and authority possessed only by God. John 1:1–2, 14 straightforwardly identifies Jesus as God:

> In the beginning was the Word, and the Word was with God, and the Word was God. He was in the beginning with God. . . . And the Word became flesh and dwelt among us . . .

There are subtler New Testament expressions that claim Jesus is God. Jesus has the power to forgive sins, a prerogative of God alone (Mark 2:1–12). John 5:21 unambiguously asserts, "For as the

Father raises the dead and gives them life, so also the Son gives life to whom he will." Jesus had the power to raise the dead and grant life—a power only the creator of life would have (cf. John 11:43). Jesus claimed to be one with the Father (John 10:30) and that "the Father is in me and I am in the Father" (John 10:38).

The New Testament writers go beyond even these verses to equate Jesus with the God of the Old Testament. There are several instances where they will quote an Old Testament verse about the God of Israel, but swap Jesus for God when they do so. For example, in Joel 2:32 we read, "And it shall come to pass that everyone who calls on the name of the LORD shall be saved." The word LORD (in small caps) is the divine name, Yahweh. Yet when Paul quotes this passage, he identifies the one to call on and be saved as Jesus:

> If you confess with your mouth that *Jesus is Lord* and believe in your heart that God raised him from the dead, you will be saved. . . . For *everyone who calls on the name of the Lord will be saved.* (Rom. 10:9, 13)

Jesus *isn't* the Father, but that fact is no obstacle to his deity. The New Testament claims that Jesus isn't God the Father, but he is indeed God.

CHAPTER 44

Just as Jesus Is and Isn't God, the Spirit Is and Isn't Jesus

In the previous chapter, we talked about how the New Testament claims that Jesus is God, even though he isn't God the Father. The New Testament creates the same "is and isn't" relationship between Jesus and the Spirit.

Our first stop is Acts 16:6–7. In verse 6, Luke makes the comment that Paul and Timothy were "forbidden by the Holy Spirit to speak the word in Asia." In the very next verse the Holy Spirit, who is always associated with the Spirit of God in the Old Testament, is referred to as "the Spirit of Jesus." This phrase simultaneously equates Jesus with God and the Spirit with Jesus (who is God).

Paul is even more explicit in this regard. The following passages clearly identify the Spirit and Jesus:

- "I know that through your prayers and the help of the *Spirit of Jesus Christ* this will turn out for my deliverance" (Phil. 1:19).
- "You, however, are not in the flesh but in the Spirit, if in fact the *Spirit of God* dwells in you. Anyone who does not have the *Spirit of Christ* does not belong to him" (Rom. 8:9).
- "And because you are sons, God has sent the *Spirit of his Son* into our hearts, crying, 'Abba! Father!'" (Gal. 4:6).

- "Now *the Lord is the Spirit*, and where the *Spirit of the Lord* is, there is freedom. And we all, with unveiled face, beholding the glory of the Lord, are being transformed into the same image from one degree of glory to another. For this comes from *the Lord who is the Spirit*" (2 Cor. 3:17–18).

The importance of this phenomenon should not be undervalued. It shows that the deity of the Holy Spirit is a doctrine based on more than pronouns (i.e., referring to the Spirit as a person; e.g., 1 Cor. 11:12) and the sporadic interchange of the Spirit with God (cf. Acts 5:3–4). Rather, as Jesus and the Father are identified with each other, so the Spirit and Jesus are identified with each other.

Since Jesus is the point of reference in both identifications, and since the Father, Son, and the Spirit are elsewhere distinguished (e.g., Matt. 28:19–20; 2 Cor. 13:14), the resulting theology is that God exists in three persons who share the same identity or essence. The *scriptural* coidentification of God, Jesus, and the Spirit are what produce Trinitarianism. The doctrine is therefore neither a guess nor the contrivance of later church history. It's scripturally grounded.

CHAPTER 45

Just Because You Can't Grasp a Doctrine Doesn't Justify Denying That Doctrine

Let's be honest. The idea of a Trinity is not fully comprehensible. How can God be one and yet three? Many people reject the idea because it seems impossible. I'd suggest it's equally incoherent to argue that something doesn't exist because you can't understand it. Quantum physics informs us that two particles of light separated by millions of miles (really, any distance) are nevertheless connected to each other. That makes absolutely no sense, yet scientific experiments have verified that it's true.

While the word "Trinity" doesn't derive from a specific Hebrew or Greek biblical word, the biblical writers subtly communicate the idea of a Trinitarian Godhead throughout the New Testament.

The Great Commission refers to baptizing people in the name of the Father, Son, and Holy Spirit (Matt. 28:19–20). The Gospel of John has several threefold descriptions of the Father, Son, and Spirit (John 1:33–34; 14:16, 26; 15:26; 16:7, 13–15; 20:21–22; cf. 1 John 4:2, 13–14). Peter's sermon at Pentecost is similar in that regard (Acts 2:33, 38): "[Jesus was] therefore exalted at the right hand of God, and having received from the Father the promise of the Holy Spirit, he has poured out this that you yourselves are seeing and hearing. . . ." And Peter said to them, 'Repent and be baptized every one of you in the name of Jesus Christ for the forgiveness of your sins, and you will receive the gift of the Holy Spirit.'"

This threefold formulaic language is present in the Epistles. In his first letter to the Corinthians, Paul's discussion of spiritual gifts connects the concept to all three persons: "Now there are varieties of gifts, but the same Spirit; and there are varieties of service, but the same Lord [Jesus]; and there are varieties of activities, but it is the same God who empowers them all in everyone" (1 Cor. 12:4–6). Paul's departing words in 2 Corinthians 13:14 read, "The grace of the Lord Jesus Christ and the love of God and the fellowship of the Holy Spirit be with you all." Peter describes believers as those "according to the foreknowledge of God the Father, in the sanctification of the Spirit, for obedience to Jesus Christ and for sprinkling with his blood" (1 Peter 1:2). Jude exhorts his readers as follows: "But you, beloved, building yourselves up in your most holy faith and praying in the Holy Spirit, keep yourselves in the love of God, waiting for the mercy of our Lord Jesus Christ that leads to eternal life" (vv. 20–21).

It's illogical to suggest that in all these passages (and more) the writers would not have wanted readers to sense that God, Jesus, and the Spirit were, in some sense, equivalent. If they had wanted to avoid this understanding, it stands to reason they'd have been more careful.

CHAPTER 46

There Are Two Ways to Think about the Three Persons of the Godhead

Trinitarianism is the Christian doctrine that God is one—he is a single, unique deity—and yet he exists eternally in three persons—Father, Son, and Holy Spirit. In my experience, a short definition like that one doesn't help people much. Some things in theology are better described than defined. To that end, theologians have typically talked about the Trinity from two perspectives that help to think about God's unity and a three-person Godhead.

One perspective is ontological. Ontology is a word that refers to a thing's *being* or essence—what a thing *is*. The "ontological Trinity" is therefore focused on God's essence and, more specifically, that each person of the Trinity is of identical essence to the others. The ontological perspective affirms that all three persons are equal in essence. That is, Jesus is as much God as the Father, and the Spirit is no less God than the Father and the Son. In terms of ontology—what the three persons are—there is no rank among them. They are all equally and fully the same in essence.

Since the three persons are equal in essence, the ontological perspective helps us avoid language that would suggest the Father, Son, and Spirit are separate deities (called tritheism), a doctrine for which Mormonism is known. It also helps us avoid the error of modalism—that the Father, Son, and Holy Spirit are merely three "modes" or expressions of the one divine essence. Passages that have the three persons simultaneously present undermine modalism (e.g., Matt. 3:13–17).

A second perspective focuses on what each person of the Godhead does in relation to the other two in terms of function. Theologians use the phrase "economic Trinity" when talking about the Godhead in this way. Each person of the Trinity has certain roles in God's interaction with the world and his plan of salvation. These roles do not occur one at a time; they often overlap. But difference in role doesn't mean disunity of essence.

As a result, the persons of the Trinity function in relation to each other. The "economic" approach helps us comprehend certain passages of Scripture that describe the actions of two or more members of the Trinity. Scripture contains implicitly hierarchical descriptions of the persons of the Trinity—where one appears subordinate to the other. For example, Jesus prayed to the Father and was in submission to his will (Matt. 26:39, 42). The Holy Spirit can be "sent" by the Father (Ps. 104:30), implying a master-servant relationship. Jesus took direction from the Spirit. Recall that, after his baptism, it was the Spirit that compelled Jesus to go into the wilderness (Mark 1:12).

Ultimately, the idea of a Trinity isn't fully comprehensible. We cannot relate anything in our experience to the way the Bible talks about God as Father, Son, and Spirit.

CHAPTER 47

Don't Assume the Doctrine of the Incarnation Is Easy to Grasp

One of the fundamental doctrines of Christianity is the deity of Christ, the doctrine that the God of the Bible came to earth as a man, born of a woman. Theologians refer to this as the incarnation. Without this doctrine, there would be no doctrine of the Trinity and no basis for what happened on the cross to be an eternal solution for the sinfulness of humanity. Only God is eternal, so you need the incarnation.

You would think, given its centrality to biblical theology, that everyone in the early years of Christianity would have fully embraced the doctrine of the incarnation. Amazingly, that isn't the case. It's not that Scripture is unclear on the matter. Rather, some people didn't want to believe it. They thought it was too great a condescension for God to make. Others just couldn't wrap their minds around it. Before we condemn anyone too quickly, think about it for a moment. *How* could God be conceived in a woman's womb, gestate for nine months, travel down the birth canal, and be born? How could *one* person be *both* God and man?

Alternative interpretations of Jesus's identity arose early in the history of Christianity. Some, such as the Ebionites, decided to reject the incarnation altogether. They argued Jesus was only a man. Ebionites thought the incarnation, which produced a Godhead, undermined monotheism. The Arians considered Jesus divine, but not coequal with the Father. As such, Jesus wasn't God incarnate but God's first and highest creation. Adoptionists argued that Jesus was merely a man but became God at some point, perhaps at his baptism or resurrection. Rather than incarnation, God entered into the man Jesus, and the result was the deification of Jesus.

On the other side, there were groups who embraced the full deity of Jesus but denied his humanity. Docetism (from the Greek verb *dokeō*, "to seem or appear") asserted that Jesus only *seemed* to be human. Apollinarianism didn't go quite so far. Instead of denying Jesus was human, Apollinarianism suggested that the divine Jesus took on genuine aspects of human nature but not the complete human nature. Nestorians taught that two distinct persons, one human and the other God, were inside Jesus, who therefore could not be equated with God. The Monophysites said the incarnation eradicated the human nature, denying Jesus's humanity.

Christian sects argued for and against these positions for centuries. Certain verses were relied on for each view (to the neglect or omission of other verses). Eventually, a consensus commitment to *all verses* emerged, embracing the entirety of biblical teaching on Jesus. The Councils of Nicaea (AD 325) and Chalcedon (AD 451) produced the teaching that Jesus was fully God and fully man, that there were two natures in one person.

CHAPTER 48

God Was Never Dumb

> I, wisdom, dwell with prudence, and I find knowledge and discretion. . . . The LORD possessed me at the beginning of his work, the first of his acts of old. Ages ago I was set up, at the first, before the beginning of the earth. When there were no depths I was brought forth, when there were no springs abounding with water. Before the mountains had been shaped, before the hills, I was brought forth. . . . When he assigned to the sea its limit, so that the waters might not transgress his command, when he marked out the foundations of the earth, then I was beside him, like a master workman. (Prov. 8:12, 22–25, 29–30)

Proverbs 8 is one of those passages everyone has read but no one seems to see the words. The speaker is Wisdom (personified). Elsewhere in Proverbs Wisdom is cast as a woman (Prov. 7:4; 8:1; 9:1). Proverbs 8:30 says that, at the time of creation, Lady Wisdom was beside God, "like a master workman." Why should you care? Lady Wisdom is portrayed as God's cocreator or agent of creation—the role assigned to Jesus in the New Testament (Col. 1:16; 1 Cor. 8:6).

In Luke 11:46–51, Jesus scolds the Pharisees and says, "The Wisdom of God said, 'I will send them prophets and apostles, some of whom they will kill and persecute'" (Luke 11:49). In Matthew's parallel account of the scolding, Jesus gets that line: "I send you prophets and wise men and scribes, some of whom you will kill and crucify" (Matt. 23:34). The gospel writers interchange Wisdom and Jesus! What's going on?

Proverbs 8 is well known to biblical scholars. The reason for the feminine language is that the Hebrew word for wisdom (*chokmah*) is grammatically feminine. Wisdom has no real (biological) gender. Consequently, there's no problem with New Testament writers thinking of Jesus as cocreator instead of Wisdom. The problem is Proverbs 8:22, where Wisdom says, "The Lord possessed me at the beginning of his work." The word translated "possessed" in the ESV is *qanah*, which elsewhere means "create" (Gen. 14:19, 22) or "obtain" (Prov. 1:5). If Jesus is the cocreator, and New Testament writers identify Jesus with wisdom, then Wisdom (and Jesus) can't be created, or else the doctrine of the Trinity is false.

Proverbs 8 was part of the discussion of Christology in the early church. It was noted that the verb *qanah* can also mean "bring forth" or "produce." But which one is the best choice in Proverbs 8:22? The debate came down to two simple questions: Was there ever a time when God lacked wisdom? And how could God be God if he lacked wisdom? You can't have the eternal God of the Bible without the attribute of wisdom. Yet God can "bring forth" the already existing second person of the Trinity as his wisdom personified, as the agent of creation.

CHAPTER 49

God Won't Allow Human Evil or Ineptitude to Overturn His Plans

Adam and Eve's sin signaled that humanity failed the test. They used the freedom God shared with them to bring rebellion into God's home and the world he created. Although God foresaw the outcome, he deemed the creation of humanity to be worth this tragic eventuality. On top of that, God foresaw something else: the situation wasn't going to get better.

The rest of the biblical saga after the failure in Eden is about reestablishing Eden despite human freedom to rebel. In doing so, he doesn't eradicate human freedom. Instead he influences people through his Spirit, other spiritual beings, and other people. He also intervenes to make sure that, no matter how great a shadow evil casts, there will always be a handful of people whose loyalty is to him.

In biblical theology, this phenomenon is called remnant theology. If you think about it, God has always been in the business of ensuring that his plan to restore Eden—his good rule in his created world—never dies. At the time of the flood, the wickedness of humanity had overspread the earth (Gen. 6:5), but Noah found grace in God's sight (Gen. 6:8). A while after the flood, the people of the world refused to spread out to fulfill the original Edenic command (Gen. 9:1; cf. Gen. 11:1–9). God scattered and disinherited them from a relationship with him (Gen. 11:1–9) and then called Abraham to keep the plan going (Gen. 12). God saved the remnant from famine in the days of Joseph, from bondage in the days of Moses, from reenslavement in the days of the judges after the failed conquest, and from extermination in exile after the nation had defected and gone after other gods.

Remnant theology framed why, centuries after rescue from exile, the people of God spurned Jesus as the Messiah. How? Paul explains, in concert with the Old Testament (Isa. 45:22; 49:6), that the remnant whom God would send his messiah to save included Gentiles. As Paul wrote, "It is not as though the word of God has failed. For not all who are descended from Israel belong to Israel, and not all are children of Abraham because they are his offspring" (Rom. 9:6–7). But the Jews also were not totally rejected. Remnant theology would carry on. In Romans 11:4–5 Paul drove that point home by quoting 1 Kings 19:18: "'I have kept for myself seven thousand men who have not bowed the knee to Baal.' So too at the present time there is a remnant, chosen by grace."

Remnant theology teaches us that God sovereignly sustains his plan. So take heart. No matter how fast the world seems to be abandoning sanity and careening toward oblivion, spiritual and otherwise, God will never let the rebellion of lesser beings thwart his purposes.

CHAPTER 50

Jesus as God and Man: Addition or Subtraction?

One of the more controversial passages in the New Testament is Philippians 2:5–8, even among Christians who believe firmly that Jesus was God in human flesh. The passage says,

> Have this mind among yourselves, which is yours in Christ Jesus, who, though he was in the form of God, did not count equality with God a thing to be grasped, but emptied himself, by taking the form of a servant, being born in the likeness of men. And being found in human form, he humbled himself by becoming obedient to the point of death, even death on a cross.

Verse 7 is the focus of the controversy. Just what does it mean for Jesus to empty himself and "taking the form of a servant, being in the likeness of men"? Does this verse teach that when the second person of the Trinity came to earth as Jesus, he emptied himself of some of the attributes of deity (e.g., omniscience, omnipotence, or omnipresence)?

The view that Jesus was in fact lacking certain attributes—by his own choice, due to a presumed "emptying"—is known as the *kenosis* view of the incarnation. The term comes from the Greek verb translated "emptied" in Phil. 2:7 (*kenoō*). This view might seem obvious on the surface. After all, Jesus couldn't be everywhere at the same time (omnipresence). He needed sleep (Mark 4:38) and of course could die, both of which are inconsistent with omnipotence. Jesus also didn't know certain things (Matt. 11:27), which defies omniscience. However, if the kenosis approach is correct—that Jesus gave up some attributes of God—how can we really speak of Jesus as fully God?

Philippians 2:6 makes it pretty clear that Jesus possessed all divine attributes prior to coming to earth. He was equal with God. This equality is described as being in the "form" of God. The same word used in the next verse ("form of a servant"). "Form" in verse 6 *can't* mean lesser than God (i.e., that Jesus gave the impression he was God but really wasn't). It also can't mean that Jesus wasn't really a servant in verse 7 either. If he was anything, he was certainly a servant. Both God and servant must be full realities.

The answer to this is a mathematical one. Is Philippians 2 saying attributes of deity were *subtracted* when Jesus became a man or that humanity was *added* to deity? *Kenosis* theory views the language as a subtraction. But if Jesus was equal to God and truly a servant, then Paul is describing the addition of humanity to deity. This addition doesn't result in the loss of attributes, but being in a human body would lead to their limitation. And that was voluntary. Jesus didn't voluntarily lop off a few attributes of deity. He voluntarily became a man, giving up *the full exercise* of those attributes.

CHAPTER 51

Even Trinitarians Fight over the Trinity

During the Middle Ages, Christianity was the dominant religion of Europe and the Mediterranean, a geographical expanse inherited from the Roman Empire. The empire had legalized Christianity in AD 313 (Constantine's Edict of Milan) and then made Nicene Christianity the official religion of the empire in AD 381 (by decree of Theodosius I).

Recall that it was the Council of Nicaea in AD 325 that resulted in the declaration of the full deity of Jesus and, consequently, the Trinity. The Nicene Creed asserted that Jesus and the Father were "of the same (*homoousios*) essence." The major competing view was known as Arianism, which claimed that Jesus wasn't fully God and was instead God's first and highest creation. The Nicene Creed also declared that the third person of the Trinity, the Holy Spirit, "proceeded from the Father." The language about the Spirit comes from John 15:26 ("the Spirit of truth, who proceeds from the Father").

That Trinitarian language was embraced at large by all Christians—until AD 1054. Some religious authorities thought the Nicene language needed a boost to reinforce the deity of Jesus. As a result, the Latin word *filioque* was inserted into the declaration that the Spirit "proceeded from the Father" to read "proceeded from the Father *and from the Son*." But this apparently innocuous decision, designed to reinforce the deity of Jesus by tightening his identification with the Father, contributed to the split of the global Christian church at the time into eastern and western factions. The former we know as Eastern Orthodoxy; the latter is Roman Catholicism.

Christian leaders in the eastern part of the Roman empire rejected the *filioque* insertion, arguing that the language was not scriptural on the basis of John 15:26. But it's instructive to look at the whole of John 15:26:

> But when the Helper comes, whom I will send to you from the Father, the Spirit of truth, who proceeds from the Father, he will bear witness about me.

While it's certainly true that the verse doesn't say the Spirit "proceeds from the Son," the verse does have Jesus (the speaker) saying that he would *send* "the Helper," who is later identified as the Holy Spirit. John 16:7 echoes this language where Jesus says, "If I do not go away, the Helper will not come to you. But if I go, *I will send him* to you."

It's difficult for many today to believe that the simple insertion of a word into the Nicene Creed, especially when it has at least implicit support from Scripture, would split global Christianity. There's certainly more to the story. The East resented the papal authority imposed on them by the West. That issue was more substantive, but the theological issues became a pretext for the split. The two branches of the church remain separate today.

CHAPTER 52

God's Decrees and His Intentions Are Not Synonymous

In earlier essays I noted how we at times misunderstand concepts like election, foreknowledge, and predestination. Those misunderstandings contribute to others, like the presumption that whatever God intends will come to pass. Scripture is very clear that divine intentions are not like divine decrees. They may be related, but they are not interchangeable synonyms. God's intentions are malleable; their actual outcomes depend on conditions that God himself sets. Take Jeremiah 18:1–10, for example:

> The word that came to Jeremiah from the LORD: "Arise, and go down to the potter's house, and there I will let you hear my words." So I went down to the potter's house, and there he was working at his wheel. And the vessel he was making of clay was spoiled in the potter's hand, and he reworked it into another vessel, as it seemed good to the potter to do."
>
> Then the word of the LORD came to me: "O house of Israel, can I not do with you as this potter has done? declares the LORD. Behold, like the clay in the potter's hand, so are you in my hand, O house of Israel. If at any time I declare concerning a nation or a kingdom, that I will pluck up and break down and destroy it, and if that nation, concerning

> which I have spoken, turns from its evil, I will relent of the disaster that I intended to do to it. And if at any time I declare concerning a nation or a kingdom that I will build and plant it, and if it does evil in my sight, not listening to my voice, then I will relent of the good that I had intended to do to it."

Zealous predestinarians love to invoke the potter and the clay illustration as though the outcomes are inevitable (Rom. 9:19–23). But one of the passages Paul alludes to in Romans 9 is Jeremiah 18. It's quite clear that, while the potter certainly has power over the clay and can do what he wants (Jer. 18:4–6), he nevertheless allows the clay a choice in its own destiny, so to speak. God can intend to destroy a nation (and so, a person), but if it repents, he will relent (Jer. 18:7–8). Conversely, he can purpose to bless, but if rebellion occurs, the Lord can alter his plan and either withhold blessing or destroy (Jer. 18:9–10). God isn't "locked in" by his intentions or purposes. He can alter his plans at will, just as the potter can improvise his intentions for the clay.

This passage certainly isn't an isolated instance. God can and does relent (Ex. 32:14; 1 Chron. 21:15; Jonah 3:9–10). Such instances show us that God is responsive to his human imagers, whom he granted freedom so they could be like him. Not everything God desires is decreed or predestined.

PART 6

HUMAN NATURE

CHAPTER 53

You Aren't a Body, Soul, and Spirit

In the context of theology, the term "anthropology" refers to doctrinal items related to humankind and the human condition. One example is the theological question of whether a human being is composed of three parts (body, soul, and spirit) or two (body and soul-spirit).

The Old Testament—that part of the Bible where the creation of humankind is detailed—is the key to the matter. Genesis 2:7 makes it clear that human beings began as a body that needed to be animated. The act of God giving animate life to the physical body is described as God "breathing" life into Adam. Thereafter the animate life of human beings and the activities we associate with consciousness are described with a range of Hebrew terms. The most frequent are *nephesh* and *ruach*, translated most often in English Bibles as "soul" and "spirit" respectively. Many Christians think these two terms are separate parts of a person.

If spirit and soul were distinct parts, one would expect them to be kept distinct in the biblical text. But that is precisely what does *not* happen. Both *nephesh* and *ruach* are used to describe the life force of a person and the faculties of the inner life:

This overlapping usage—and it is only a sampling—strongly suggests that soul and spirit should be understood as soul-spirit, the immaterial part of a human being. This is the anthropology inherited by the New Testament writers.

	nephesh	*ruach*
Animate life; the act of breathing to display life (includes animal life)	Gen. 1:20–21, 24, 30; 12:13; 19:19; 35:18; Ex. 4:19; Job 11:20	Gen. 6:17; 7:15, 22; Job 7:7; Ps. 135:17; Zech. 12:1 (note that *ruach* is also interchanged with *nishmat*, the word for "breath" in Gen. 2:7; Isa. 42:5; 57:16)
Source or seat of emotions	Gen. 34:3, 8; 42:21; Ex. 15:19; 23:19; Lev. 26:15, 30, 43; 1 Sam. 1:10, 15; 2 Sam. 5:8; 17:8; 2 Kings 4:27; Job 14:22; Pss. 6:3; 13:2; 23:3; 35:25; 42:1–2; Jer. 13:17; 14:19; Lam. 3:17	Num. 5:14; 5:30; 2 Chron. 18:22; Prov. 14:29; Eccl. 10:4; Isa. 54:6; 57:15;
Volitional will; decision-making capacity; attitudes; inner disposition; self-awareness	Lev. 26:16; Deut. 4:29; 6:5; 10:12; 14.26; 21:14; 23:24; Judg. 16:16; 1 Sam. 2:33; 23:20; Pss. 42:6; 107:26; Prov. 19:2	Ex. 6:9; Num. 14:24; Josh. 2:11; 5:1; Ezra 1:1; Job 32:18; Pss. 34:19; 51:19; 76:13; Prov. 15:13; 16:19; 17:22, 27; 18:14; 29:23; Isa. 19:3; 29:14; 57:15; 61:3; Jer. 51:11; Hag. 1:14;

There are only two verses that seem to split up these terms (Heb. 4:12; 1 Thess. 5:23). But these passages are best seen not as a contradiction to the contrary mass of evidence in the Old Testament. In both cases, the wording expresses totality of being, not distinct parts.

CHAPTER 54

Scripture Is Silent on the Origin of the Soul

The Bible doesn't provide answers to all the questions we'd like answered. For example, it doesn't address when and how each human soul comes into existence. Historically, theologians have offered three answers to these questions.

One view of the soul's origin is called *traducianism* (or generationism). This view posits that the soul, the immaterial part of a human person, is created by the human parents at the moment of fertilization/conception. In other words, the soul comes about through the normal act of procreation or "natural generation." Passages that describe the formation of the fetus in the womb are sometimes used to defend this view (Job 10:8–12; Ps. 139:13–16). But such passages never actually describe (or explain) how something nonmaterial can be created by a material process. Other passages like Hebrews 7:10, which has Levi being "in the loins" of his ancestor Abraham, are also offered in defense. But it is biologically impossible for a full human being to be inside a male. A human being is made at conception when genetic material from both a man and woman are united—inside a woman, not a man. Therefore, Hebrews 7:10 likely isn't speaking to this issue.

A second view is referred to as *creationism* (not to be confused with the creationism that refers to God's act of creation of the heavens and the earth). Creationism denies that the soul is made by the parents through procreation. Rather, it asserts that God directly and specially creates each individual soul right after conception and then implants it into the conceptus. For many this view seems like a workable alternative to the fundamental problem of traducianism, that a nonmaterial thing is created by material means. But this view is rejected by many Christians because this view has God making a sinful soul and then implanting it, as long as you assume that each soul has inherited Adam's guilt (Rom. 5:12). This idea lacks specific scriptural defense and would seem nullified by other passages on the holy nature of God's character.

The third perspective is rarely held today but was at one time deemed plausible (in some form or another) by several Christian theologians. This view, called the preexistence view, argues that all souls were created by God long before the creation of humanity, and therefore preexisted before being sent to inhabit the body God providentially assigned to them. Since souls in this view were created sinless, the problem of creationism is avoided. However, the view fails for those who take Romans 5:12 as evidence that each human is born with a sinful soul, guilty before God, because of Adam's fall. Preexistence has no direct biblical support, although Jeremiah 1:5 and Job 15:8 are sometimes read as evidence for the idea that the first man born was already present in God's council before being born on earth. This view was widely condemned in the early Middle Ages.

The truth is that Scripture does not provide sufficient information to draw a firm conclusion about the origin of the soul. God is under no obligation to satisfy every point of our curiosity. This mystery is of less significance than the one God chose to reveal after long ages of time, "the mystery of his will, according to his purpose, which he set forth in Christ as a plan for the fullness of time, to unite all things in him, things in heaven and things on earth" (Eph. 1:9).

CHAPTER 55

The Image of God Refers to What We Are, Not Something Put into Us

The words of Genesis 1:26 are some of the most well-known in the Old Testament: "Let us create humankind in our image and as our likeness." They're also some of the most debated. If you looked up the passage in serious commentaries and theology books, you'd discover that just about everyone and his uncle has an interpretation for what the words mean.

If we read the passage closely (Gen. 1:26–28) and move past English translation to the Hebrew text, the answer as to what the "image" means becomes clear. Whatever the image is, it is unique to humankind and not shared with any other part of the earthly creation. It is also equally and fully possessed by all humans, and it's not incrementally bestowed. When Adam and Eve had children, the text assumes the image was passed on (Gen. 5:3). Genesis 9:6 indicates that all humans after Adam and Eve were also in God's image.

These observations are crucial, for they mean that any definition of the image that is ability-based cannot be correct. The reason is simple: the fertilized egg created at human conception has no abilities, even though it is fully human. Since the image is nowhere described as incrementally gained, the idea that the contents of the womb gain the image at some point in development is disallowed.

The Bible knows nothing of humans being potentially or partially in God's image. Humanity is God's image.

But what does that mean? The answer comes from Hebrew grammar. The key phrase is that humankind was created *in* God's image. As is the case in English, Hebrew prepositions convey many different nuances of meaning. To illustrate in English, if I say, "Put the dishes *in* the sink," the preposition speaks to *location*. For "I broke the mirror *in* pieces," and "I wrote the letter *in* pencil," the preposition describes *result* and the *means* by which something is done. However, the phrase "I work *in* medicine" means that I work *as* a doctor, physician's assistant, nurse, or even a research scientist. The preposition denotes *function* or *role*.

So it is with the phrase in Genesis 1:26. To be created *in* God's image means to be created *as* God's image. The effect of the translation is significant. There is no sense of gaining the image in stages. *To be human is to be God's image.* That's a description that applies to all human life, no matter the stage of development. Ultimately, this means humans function as God's representation. We were put on earth to function in God's place—to steward his creation as though he were physically present. We may not be able to discern what God wants each person to be or do, especially those who are handicapped or whose lives are cut off prematurely. But the imaging idea informs all of biblical ethics. It also describes our Christian lives: we are to image Jesus, who is the ultimate imager of God (Rom. 8:29; 1 Cor. 15:49; 2 Cor. 3:18).

CHAPTER 56

God Is unlike Anything That Exists on Earth, except for Us

One of the fundamental truths of Scripture is that God is incomparable. After the miraculous crossing of the sea, Moses asked, "Who is like you, O LORD, among the gods?" (Ex. 15:11). The psalmist echoed the thought in Psalm 89:6, "For who in the skies can be compared to the LORD? Who among the heavenly beings is like the LORD?" God himself puts forth the obvious answer: "I am God, and there is none like me" (Isa. 46:9).

The irony of all this is that, according to Scripture, there is something in God's earthly creation that is like him, by his own design: humankind. Genesis 5:1–2 says it very plainly: "When God created man, he made him in the likeness of God. Male and female he created them" (cf. Gen. 1:26–27).

What does it mean to be like God? In a broad sense, it means that we are God's imagers. But more pointedly, the notion of being like God means that we share God's attributes. *We are like him.*

Theologians typically classify the attributes of God into two categories: those that are communicable (shared with humanity) and those that are incommunicable (not shared with humanity). Examples of the former would be love and intelligence. Theologians often propose attributes like eternity and omnipresence for the latter.

However, this language is imprecise. No communicable attribute is completely shared with us. We share such attributes only partially, to a much lesser degree than God. Even some incommunicable attributes are at least reflected in humanity. We are not eternal, but if we believe, we will have everlasting life with God, sharing his life forever. As a result, it's probably better to think of communicable attributes as those attributes we share with God more than others, and incommunicable attributes as those we share the least, or may reflect because of the way he will transform us in the eternal state.

The takeaway here isn't two new words for our doctrine vocabulary. It's the realization that, out of all earthly creation, only humanity can legitimately claim to be like God. Human life is therefore special to God; it has a sacred status. That status is why, for example, God declared that anyone who takes an innocent human life must forfeit their own life "for God made man in his own image" (Gen. 9:6). If God holds human life in such high esteem, the least we can do is imitate the one who first shared his life with us as we navigate our relationships with others.

CHAPTER 57

You're a Sinner Because You're Not God

Perhaps the most significant point of doctrine that gets misarticulated from Romans 5:12 is the notion that all humans inherit *guilt* before God because of what happened in Eden. Though this is common Christian teaching, the passage never says that:

> So then, just as sin entered the world through one man and death through sin, and so death spread to all people with the result that all sinned. (NET)

Romans 5:12 doesn't say that, from Adam onward, all humans are born guilty before God, something many theologians presume results from Adam's "original sin." It may sound surprising, but no passage in the Old Testament ever looks back to Eden as an explanation for humanity's guilt before God.

That is not to say, however, that all humans do not need the saving work of Christ to have eternal life (they certainly do) or that humans merit salvation in any way (they certainly do not). Rather, humans become guilty before God not because of what someone else (Adam) did, but because of what *they* do and cannot avoid doing. All humans, if permitted to live (e.g., are not stillborn) and possessing the mental faculties for willfully transgressing the will and standards of God, will offend God and incur guilt that can only be forgiven through faith in the gospel of Jesus Christ.

Romans 5:12 clearly says that the result of what Adam did was death. Adam began to die the moment he was expelled from Eden and the presence of God, the source of life. When we die, our immaterial self is permanently separated from our body. That is the death all humans experience (unless they're present at the Lord's return; 1 Thess. 4:16–18). But there is a "second death" (Rev. 20:6, 14; 21:8) that unbelievers suffer, namely, eternal separation from the presence of God.

Universally, humans sin. As imagers of God who share his attributes, Adam and Eve had freedom. They chose to sin. Even in the very presence of God they showed themselves lesser than God. All of us are born outside God's immediate presence and are far less than the God we image. We are not perfect moral beings like God, who always uses his freedom in holiness and righteousness. We all sin and cannot escape sinning. That is our lot because of Adam—*but our guilt is our own.*

The lone exception was Jesus, whose genealogy runs through Adam (Luke 3:38). Jesus was truly man and truly God. If the point of Romans 5:12 is that all humans inherit guilt via Adam, then Jesus, despite never sinning, must have inherited guilt because he was human. The virgin birth doesn't exempt him; his mother was human. Jesus wasn't inserted into Mary's womb with no genetic relationship to her. Paul claims that Jesus truly descended from David "after the flesh" (Rom. 1:3), not just legally.

Like us, Jesus inherited that which Romans 5:12 says extended from Adam's fall: mortality. But unlike us, he did not sin against God. Though mortal like us, he was also God, which we are not. And it's a good thing, because in his mortality, the sinless Jesus would die in our place (2 Cor. 5:21). Because he could die he could suffer the penalty of our sin. But because he was also God, his sacrifice was untainted and eternal, and he would conquer death so that all who believe might live with him forever.

CHAPTER 58

Can Unbelievers Please God?

Everyone reading this book is a sinner. No human being has ever been capable of living a sinless life, except Jesus Christ, who was also God. Paul describes the natural estate of humanity as one where we "live in the passions of our flesh, carrying out the desires of the body and mind," thus incurring (and deserving) the wrath of God (Eph. 2:3). Because we sin, we are "sons of disobedience" (Eph. 2:2). Until we believe and have Christ's righteousness put to our account (Rom. 5:17–18, 21; Phil. 3:9), which unites us to Jesus (Rom. 6:5; Eph. 2:13), the wrath of God remains on us (John 3:36).

In view of this situation, it's no wonder that I was taught in seminary that it's impossible for an unbeliever to ever do anything that pleases God. By way of illustration, one theologian puts it this way:

> "Because man is totally or pervasively corrupt, he is *incapable of changing his character or of acting in a way that is distinct from his corruption.* He is unable to discern, to love, or to choose the things that are pleasing to God."*

Several verses are offered to support this contention, most notably Romans 8:7–8: "For the mind that is set on the flesh is hostile to

* Robert L. Reymond, *A New Systematic Theology of the Christian Faith* (Nashville: Thomas Nelson, 1998), 453.

God, for it does not submit to God's law; indeed, it cannot. Those who are in the flesh cannot please God."

This idea, and its understanding of passages like Romans 8:7–8, is flatly contradicted by other passages. The story of the conversion of the gentile Cornelius in Acts 10 is perhaps the best case in point. Cornelius was a "God-fearing man," someone who respected Judaism and its God but who nevertheless had never heard the gospel. When Peter heard how Cornelius was visited by an angel who commanded Cornelius to summon the apostle to his home, Peter exclaimed, "Truly I understand that God shows no partiality, but in every nation anyone who fears him and *does what is right is acceptable to him*" (Acts 10:34–35).

The passage is clear. While no one can please God in the sense of meriting salvation, unsaved people *can* please God—they can do things that are acceptable to God. Paul said the same thing in Romans 2:14, that gentiles not possessing God's law nevertheless at times do what's in the law. It's incoherent to think that a gentile who lives in accord with God's law at any given moment is displeasing God by doing so. Romans 8:7–8 is meant to contrast those controlled by the Spirit and those controlled by the flesh, with respect to lifestyle and being a child of God. Unbelievers *can* please God. Cornelius shows us that.

PART 7

SALVATION

CHAPTER 59

For by Grace You Are Saved through Faith Without Works Is Dead

The gospel of Jesus Christ is the good news that salvation is a gift. Because we are lost, imperfect beings, we cannot earn salvation by our works. Paul famously wrote, "For by grace you are saved through faith. . . . It is a gift of God, not a result of works" (Eph. 2:8–9). John 3:16 says that whoever believes in Jesus has everlasting life; it doesn't say "whoever lives an exemplary life merits everlasting life."

Christians are, of course, aware of these verses, yet they struggle with believing that it's so simple. I've met many who are haunted by sins of the past or present. The message of the gospel is that we can do nothing to deserve salvation. We cannot earn God's favor. Salvation is a gift from God received by faith. God already loved us while we were lost in sin (Rom. 5:8) before we believed (John 3:16). It therefore makes no sense to think that our works ensure that God doesn't stop loving us. The thought is utterly illogical (and unbiblical).

But what about what James says? Many Bible students stumble at his words:

> What good is it, my brothers, if someone says he has faith but does not have works? Can that faith save him? . . . But

> someone will say, "You have faith and I have works." Show me your faith apart from your works, and I will show you my faith by my works. . . . Was not Abraham our father justified by works when he offered up his son Isaac on the altar? You see that faith was active along with his works, and faith was completed by his works . . . You see that a person is justified by works and not by faith alone. (James 2:14, 18, 21–22, 24)

It's easy to think that Paul and James disagree. But they actually don't. James isn't saying that faith is good but we need works to put us over the top and somehow merit salvation. Meriting salvation means that God *owes* it to us because of what we've done. That idea is foreign to James. Rather, *James wants to know that a person's faith is real*. Someone can profess faith and then live like a hypocrite. James isn't saying their works aren't good enough to put God in their debt—*he's saying their faith is phony*. Faith is what saves, but works are crucial to validate the reality of one's faith.

The right way to understand this relationship between faith and works is to put it this way: Works are essential to *corroborating* salvation; they are not the *meritorious cause* of salvation. That statement gives James his due and keeps him in perspective. Works must be there to certify the reality of saving faith; they don't replace or transcend faith. That's why I put the words of Paul and James together in the chapter title: "For by Grace You Are Saved through Faith Without Works Is Dead."

Salvation is by faith, but that faith is dead, nonexistent, and without works.

CHAPTER 60

No One Can Merit God's Favor

One of the great misunderstandings about Old Testament theology concerns its doctrine of salvation. Because of certain statements in the New Testament, particularly in the writings of Paul, that no one can be justified by the works of the law (Rom. 3:20), most Bible students have a firm grasp of human *inability* to merit salvation. But it would be a mistake to think that in theory salvation could be merited by perfect obedience to the law. It could not. The reason is simple. One could obey the demands of the law perfectly and still not believe. One can obey rules without having faith and without having faith in the right object.

Faith is at the heart of salvation—in both testaments. Given the impossibility of perfect obedience to the law, this makes sense. Salvation must be extended in grace by God. And it is extended on the basis of belief. This is why Paul makes Old Testament characters like Abraham (Rom. 4:1–3) and David (Rom. 4:6–8) the primary illustrations of his teaching on salvation by grace through faith, not of works (Eph. 2:8–9; Rom. 3:20–25).

Old Testament salvation was not merited by keeping the law. Rather, Old Testament salvation was about *believing loyalty*. What did Israelites need to believe? That Yahweh, their God, was the God of all gods, and that this same God had chosen to enter into a covenant relationship with Israel, Abraham's seed, in love. Those who truly believed would respond with faithfulness out of reciprocal love and gratitude, not in order to merit favor. God had already favored Israel when he offered them a relationship in the first place. Obedience was the response to God's love when one believed it, not to convince God that he ought to love.

The same is true in the New Testament. There is no possibility of meriting salvation *and no need to think that the effort is necessary.* No one puts God into debt by their goodness or obedience. God doesn't owe anyone salvation because of their works (Gal. 2:16; Rom 3:20, 28). Those who are self-deceived into thinking they can merit God's favor are doomed (Gal. 3:10). Salvation is a gift available through the death of Christ (Gal. 2:21). It is offered freely by God in response to our belief in what Jesus did (Gal. 2:21; 3:2, 5), which is actually our belief in the sincerity of God's offer, since it was all his plan anyway.

If you're a Christian, you're likely thinking you understand all this. Do you? If you feel any impulse—because of current sin or guilt from the past—that your relationship with God needs to be maintained by your good behavior ("faithfulness"), you really don't get it. You couldn't merit salvation in the first place. Christ died for you while you were in sin (Rom. 5:8). It makes no doctrinal sense that it must then be *kept* by works. Let God love you and be done with it.

CHAPTER 61

We Cannot Avoid Sinning, and We Contribute Nothing to Our Salvation

Earlier I wrote that we didn't inherit guilt from the fall, but our mortality and life outside the direct presence of God. Those realities, coupled with the fact that we aren't perfect moral beings like God, means that every human who, under providence, is born and has the ability to choose rebellion will do so without exception, save for Jesus, who was also God. We inevitably become guilty in the wake of what Adam did, but we are not rendered guilty because of his guilt.

This perspective may be new to you, given that Christian history has for so long inserted the inheritance of guilt into Romans 5:12. But many verses teach that our guilt is earned.

- "All have *sinned* and fall short of the glory of God" (Rom. 3:23).
- "None is righteous, no not one. . . . All have *turned aside*" (Rom. 3:10–11).

These verses focus on *our* guilt because of *our* sin. But our problem is deeper—it is in our very nature to sin. This does not mean we are guilty because of what Adam did. It means that, like Adam, we will rebel. Adam's sin didn't produce our condemnation, it "led to condemnation" (Rom. 5:18). Further, *there is nothing about being human that tends toward holiness and sinlessness.* Only God has such perfect quality of character. For this reason, Paul could say that we are "by nature the children of wrath" (Eph. 2:3).

David said the same thing in Psalm 51:5, "I was brought forth in iniquity, and in sin did my mother conceive me." David is not referring to the act of intercourse that resulted in his conception being sinful. There is no indication in Scripture David was illegitimate. Rather, he is thinking of his own sins and sinfulness. From the moment he was conceived and then born, he was destined to be a sinner. He was living with the guilt of his doings when he wrote this psalm. This is clear from the immediately preceding verses:

> For I know my transgressions,
> and my sin is ever before me.
> Against you, you only, have I sinned
> and done what is evil in your sight. (Ps. 51:3–4)

David felt the weight of guilt because of what he'd done, acting out his own unavoidable sinfulness, not because of some ethereal guilt he'd inherited from Adam.

Another psalm, a *miktam* of David, is important in this light:

> The wicked are estranged from the womb;
> they *go astray* from birth, speaking lies. (Ps. 58:3)

This is no indication of inherited guilt in the womb. Neither a fetus nor an infant "speaks lies." Instead, the point is consistent with that of Psalm 51: humans are born sinners, and they will invariably sin and offend God. Depravity, then, ought to be understood in terms of the inescapability of becoming guilty before God through our own inevitable rebellions. We can't blame anyone else for our need of reconciliation to God, including Adam.

CHAPTER 62

Without Sin There Is Innocence before God—and Eternal Life through the Resurrection of Christ

One of the most wrenching tragedies anyone can experience is the death of a child, whether by miscarriage, stillbirth, or later. But in circumstances where children have no capacity to understand sin and the gospel, parents can be paralyzed by the uncertainty. Those grieving over an abortion decision, or who have mentally handicapped children, face the same apparent quandary. Frankly, a flawed interpretation of Romans 5:12, so prevalent in Christianity, is partly to blame. It teaches that all humans are guilty before God from the moment of conception.

As uncomfortable as it sounds, if the traditional view of Romans 5:12 is accurate, then all such children face an eternity separate from God. That is the only logical conclusion. Pastors who suggest that God makes exceptions, or try to assert that such children are elect, or seek to assure parents that God will wipe their memories clean so that they won't grieve for their children for eternity, are misleading people, no matter how well-intentioned they are. There is absolutely no exegetical warrant from the biblical text for God turning a blind eye toward the guilty sinner apart from Christ. Passages about wiping away every tear have been ripped from their context. Those who appeal to infant baptism (whose validity they argue on the basis of circumcision) ignore the fact that election is not synonymous with salvation.

Good theology points to another perspective, and true comfort in such cases. If Romans 5:12 is not about inheriting guilt, then all people who don't knowingly and willfully choose to rebel against God aren't guilty in his sight.

This does not mean that such children go to heaven because they have merit—no human merits salvation in any way. To understand why the innocent are with the Lord one must ask why anyone suffers the "second death," eternal separation from God (Rev. 20:6, 14; 21:8). They suffer because their guilt before God hasn't been removed. Both the lost and the saved will be raised on the last day (Acts 24:15), some to everlasting life, others to everlasting contempt (Dan. 12:2). Those in the latter group are separated from God forever because their sins were never forgiven through the work of Christ. They suffer the second death.

The innocent will therefore be raised with everyone else, but *having never incurred guilt before God, they will not suffer the second death.* By default they are with the Lord—not on the basis of their innocence or even on the basis of sinlessness. They are there because of the resurrection, which only God in Christ can accomplish. Salvation of anyone, those who believe in the gospel and those without guilt who are raised, is accomplished solely by the Lord.

So take heart if you have suffered such a tragedy or know someone who has. Romans 5:12 is not an intractable pronouncement of doom. There is secure, biblical warrant for seeing these lost loved ones again.

CHAPTER 63

What Isn't Gained by Moral Perfection Can't Be Lost by Moral Imperfection

I've already devoted space to the problem of the Christian struggle with works. The flawed theology that so many believers bludgeon themselves with every day is that their standing before God, their very salvation, depends on their performance. So many can't seem to grasp that our works can't have anything to do with maintaining the gift of salvation if they had nothing to do with receiving it. The role of works is to corroborate salvation, not merit it. No one's performance puts God in their debt.

Even as Christians we sin, and the New Testament says that we will. In fact, if we say we don't sin, the Scripture says we are self-deceived liars:

> If we say we have no sin, we deceive ourselves, and the truth is not in us.... If we say we have not sinned, we make him a liar, and his word is not in us. (1 John 1:8, 10)

Time for a lesson on the obvious. *All Christians sin*. The same letter of 1 John adds that as Christians we shouldn't be unrestrained in our sinning, perpetually choosing our way against God's, since we have been born into God's family:

> No one born of God makes a practice of sinning, for God's seed abides in him, and he cannot keep on sinning because he has been born of God. (1 John 3:9)

But now for the equally obvious, and so often missed, correlation. While we were yet sinners, before we trusted the gospel, Christ died for us to reconcile us to God:

> For one will scarcely die for a righteous person—though perhaps for a good person one would dare even to die—but God shows his love for us in that while we were still sinners, Christ died for us. . . . For if while we were enemies we were reconciled to God by the death of his Son, much more, now that we are reconciled, shall we be saved by his life. (Rom. 5:7–8, 10)

Rather than feel guilty about how much we aren't like Jesus, and pledge in our hearts to "do better," we need to let the blessing of what he did, and will do, rewire the way we think. Don't turn Christlikeness into a task to perform lest God be angry with us. That's terrible theology. It turns grace into duty and snubs the grace of God. God is more interested in what you believe than your feats of obedience. To be blunt, to think that you have to maintain something by your performance that you couldn't obtain by your performance is theological illiteracy.

CHAPTER 64

If You Believe, You Are Eternally Secure, and If You Don't, You Aren't

One of the most misunderstood teachings of Scripture concerns the assurance of the believer—sometimes referred to as eternal security. The modern Christian subculture of evangelicalism has turned embracing the gospel by faith into mouthing an incantation—that thing we call the sinner's prayer. Once the magic words are whispered, you're in, no matter what you might end up believing. That just isn't how the New Testament describes the faith.

I'm not suggesting that someone can lose their salvation by committing sins. I've dealt with that in several essays already. Nothing in Scripture says that moral imperfection results in the loss of something (i.e., salvation) that could not be gained by moral perfection. That theology is contrary to grace. Paul addressed this flawed thinking in Romans 8. The God you fear will condemn you for your sins is the one who forgives and justifies:

> There is therefore now no condemnation for those who are in Christ Jesus. . . . If God is for us, who can be against us? . . . Who shall bring any charge against God's elect? It is God who justifies. (Rom. 8:1, 31, 33)

But there's a corollary to this. *God forces no one to believe.* Just as Adam was in the place God wanted him, without any sin, God allowed him to choose rebellion. God will not eradicate an imager's free will to prevent them from turning their back on his grace. This is why Paul and other New Testament writers were so concerned with believers falling into unbelief.

> [God] has now reconciled in his body of flesh by his death, in order to present you holy and blameless and above reproach before him, *if indeed you continue in the faith*, stable and steadfast, *not shifting from the hope of the gospel* that you heard. (Col. 1:22–23)

> [The Israelites] were broken off because of their *unbelief*, but you [gentiles] stand fast through faith. So do not become proud, but fear. For if God did not spare the natural branches, neither will he spare you. Note then . . . God's kindness to you, *provided you continue in his kindness. Otherwise you too will be cut off.* (Rom. 11:20–22)

> Take care, *brothers*, lest there be in any of you an evil, *unbelieving* heart, leading you to *fall away* from the living God. (Heb. 3:12)

> If we died with him, we will also live with him. If we endure, we will also reign with him. *If we deny him, he will also deny us*. If we are unfaithful, he remains faithful, since he cannot deny himself. (2 Tim. 2:11–13 NET)

In this last passage, Paul is speaking to Timothy, who is certainly a believer. But Paul's concern is denying Christ—the *rejection* of the gospel that must be believed for eternal life. We might be unfaithful in our performance, but God remains faithful in his promise of salvation. It's not about works, but grace. You can't sin away your salvation, but you can decide to turn your back on it. If you believe, you are eternally secure. If you don't, you aren't.

CHAPTER 65

You Should Think Twice about Being More Offended by the Cross than God

Most people want to be fair and be thought of as fair. We want to receive what we've earned. We don't want to be blamed for what someone else did poorly or failed to do. Fairness is the flip side of justice. Except when it's not, and that's especially the case when it comes to Jesus.

The gospel of Jesus Christ is the story of how Jesus, the son of God and God incarnate, died on the cross for the sins of the world (John 1:29; 3:16). In other words, it's the story of how Jesus died in our place. As sinners we deserved death (Rom. 6:23). But incredibly, Christ died on our behalf (Rom. 5:5–8). As Paul puts it, "For our sake [God] made [Jesus] to be sin who knew no sin, so that in him we might become the righteousness of God" (2 Cor. 5:21; cf. 1 Peter 1:18–19; 3:18). That's hardly fair.

It's because of God's unfairness—putting our sins on the sinless Jesus and its violent outcome, Jesus's death in the place of the guilty—that many people, even Christians, are repulsed by the concept of substitutionary ("vicarious") atonement. In response, some revise or reject the doctrine.

The result of such thinking is awkward. Proponents believe themselves to be more just and fair-minded than God. To them, making someone, especially Jesus, suffer for something he never did seems to be unjust. But that objection is hollow. It's true that God planned to save humanity from sin in this way. It's equally true that Jesus *volunteered* (1 Tim. 2:6; Gal. 2:20; Phil. 2:1–8; Heb. 10:5–7).

The notion of blood substitution in response to the defilement of sin has deep Old Testament roots. Israelites who became ritually impure, whether accidentally or by the consequence of certain sins, were required to offer an animal sacrifice to once again approach God on holy ground (Lev. 4–5). The Passover lamb, while not a sin offering, illustrated for Israelites that God would shield them from the last plague upon Egypt and its pharaoh for their sins—refusing God's command to release his people. This is why Paul refers to Jesus as the Passover lamb (1 Cor. 5:7). It is also why the author of Hebrews sets his discussion about Jesus's sacrifice being greater than animal sacrifices in the tabernacle and holy of holies.

Any view of the atonement that excludes substitution ignores the direct statements to the contrary in Scripture and neglects comparisons between Jesus's death in New Testament and Old Testament sacrifices. The purpose of those comparisons is to show us how our sins will not be added to our account. There can be no forgiveness without payment for sin.

CHAPTER 66

Don't Fall for the False Dilemma Fallacy When You Think about the Atonement

I've never quite understood why so many Christians are suspicious of logical thinking. I've encountered students who think that approaching the Bible logically is a covert attempt to confuse them or steer them to "liberalism"! Logical thinking is about being clear and precise. When it comes to theology, logical thought can help cut through a lot of distracting talk. The seemingly endless debate about the atonement is a case in point.

Historically, there has been a lot of disagreement about the meaning of the atonement. That's still the case. Much of the debate stems from a disdain for substitutionary atonement (also known as "penal substitution"). Let's look at some alternatives.

One option is the *Ransom Theory*, which argues that the death of Christ was a ransom paid to Satan. Since Satan is lord of the dead in biblical theology, and all humans die, Satan had legal claim to every soul. The sacrifice of Jesus paid the price—the ransom. This view usually offers "ransom" language found in several verses as support (Matt. 20:28; 1 Tim. 2:6). Although there was a price to be paid for sin (Rom. 6:23), the Bible never specifically says that Satan was *owed* that price. Another alternative is the *Moral Influence Theory*, which asserts that the death of Christ was not a substitutionary sacrifice to cancel sin's penalty but rather an example of suffering to demonstrate God's love. The *Governmental Theory* says that what happened on the cross simply shows God's hatred of sin and satisfies God's demand for justice. The *Recapitulation Theory* says that Jesus repeated ("recapitulated") in his life and death all the stages of human life and death. The purpose was to live a life counter to Adam's disobedience to illustrate the way our lives must be transformed. There are other views, but these examples are sufficient to make the point that follows.

If you read about alternative theories of the atonement, it won't take you long to notice a pattern. It seems no matter what the view, proponents of an alternative want to convince you that your choice for getting the atonement right is to adopt their view and dispense with substitutionary atonement. In logic, that's what's known as the false dilemma fallacy (also known as the either-or fallacy). You're led to believe that you must either choose the alternative view or adopt the flawed substitutionary view, for no other choice is possible.

Nearly all theories about the atonement have some attachment to a scriptural idea, or at least one that's theologically defensible. There's no need to choose one and deny the others. We just need to make sure we don't deny some point of validity about the death of Jesus—like the fact that he died in our place, as our substitute.

CHAPTER 67

Neither Being Poor nor Helping the Poor Are Tickets to Heaven

In the Sermon on the Mount Jesus said, "Blessed are the poor in spirit, for theirs is the kingdom of heaven" (Matt. 5:3). James, the brother of Jesus wrote, "Listen, my beloved brothers, has not God chosen those who are poor in the world to be rich in faith and heirs of the kingdom, which he has promised to those who love him?" (James 2:5–6). Are the poor offered special access to the kingdom of God? Do those who help them garner special favor with God?

The answer to both those questions is no. These verses and many others have been misunderstood—or used deliberately by politicians to curry favor—for centuries. Jesus's words refer to the poor *in spirit* and therefore have nothing to do with wealth. James's statement, however, certainly speaks to personal wealth or its absence. But look closely at the wording. James says the poor who are rich in faith will inherit the kingdom. The promise is for those *who love God*. These descriptions are consistent with the real gospel that all those who place their faith in the grace of God, shown in the sacrifice of Jesus on the cross, will be saved. You can't love God and reject the sacrifice of his Son.

The biblical teaching on the poor is clear. God hates when the powerless are abused. Amos pulls no punches about God's attitude toward the piety of those who abuse and extort the poor and take bribes while turning away the needy:

> I hate, I despise your feasts,
> and I take no delight in your solemn assemblies.
> (Amos 5:21; cf. 5:10–15)

Exploitation and neglect of the needy are numbered with sins like idolatry (Ezek. 16:49; 18:12).

Sadly, too many theologians and pastors have exchanged the gospel for social uprightness and justice. Making sure that the poor are not marginalized and spurned is something God demands, but the practice of social justice isn't the gospel. Rather, social justice is what should happen when the gospel is embraced.

Neither rich nor poor are exempt from belief. There is no cause-and-effect relationship between poverty and walking with God. The same goes for the wealthy. The gospel calls for a radical faith decision: choosing not to trust in wealth and being willing to lose it or give it all away for the kingdom of God. It's an issue of the heart. John 3:16 doesn't say that "whosoever gives his wealth away shall have everlasting life." In Acts 16:30 when the Philippian jailer asked Paul and Silas, "What must I do to be saved?" the answer was not "feed the poor" or "alleviate poverty" or "become poor." The answer was crystal clear: "Believe on the Lord Jesus Christ" (Acts 16:31).

CHAPTER 68

There's No Plan B When It Comes to Eternal Life

Earlier when we talked about the problem of unbelief, we noted that Hebrews 6 says any other means of salvation besides what happened on the cross is impossible. That isn't the only passage in the Bible that makes such a point. When it comes to the biblical doctrine of salvation, all paths don't lead to eternal life.

Acts 4:10–12 is one of the clearest articulations of the exclusivity of the gospel:

> By the name of Jesus Christ of Nazareth, whom you crucified, whom God raised from the dead—by him this man is standing before you well. This Jesus is the stone that was rejected by you, the builders, which has become the cornerstone. And there is salvation in no one else, for there is no other name under heaven given among men by which we must be saved.

It's difficult to see how the thought could be communicated more clearly ("there is salvation in no one else"). And yet there are people in Christian churches who entertain the notion that one's spiritual hunger or sincerity will move God's heart to admit someone to heaven. But nothing we do merits salvation, and God has already shown he loves sinners by having Jesus die in our place. God isn't interested in our terms for salvation; he cares only about his.

Jesus himself made this same point clear. In his conversation with Nicodemus he said:

> For God so loved the world, that he gave his only Son, that whoever believes in him should not perish but have eternal life. For God did not send his Son into the world to condemn the world, but in order that the world might be saved through him.... Whoever believes in the Son has eternal life; whoever does not obey the Son shall not see life, but the wrath of God remains on him. (John 3:16–17, 36)

If that wasn't clear enough, Jesus also said, "Whoever denies me before men, I also will deny before my Father who is in heaven" (Matt. 10:33). He wasn't much of a pluralist.

Neither were Paul and Peter. The former wrote, "Therefore I endure everything for the sake of the elect, that they also may obtain the salvation that is in Christ Jesus with eternal glory.... If we deny him, he also will deny us" (2 Tim. 2:10, 12). Peter compared false teachers who "deny the Master who bought them" to the angels that sinned and were cast into the abyss, since they bring on themselves "swift destruction" (2 Peter 2:1).

I don't see any ambiguity here.

CHAPTER 69

If You Are in Christ, Satan Has No Authority over Your Eternal Destiny

The New Testament has a lot to say about the devil, most of it overtly negative. Even the term "devil" is pejorative, since the Greek word *diabolos* means "slanderer." The devil's proper name in the New Testament is Satan, a term drawn from Hebrew into the vocabulary of the New Testament that means "adversary." Occasionally, though, the New Testament says some interesting things about Satan that move beyond describing his evil character and that have doctrinal significance. Hebrews 2:14–15 is a case in point:

> [Jesus] himself likewise partook of the same things, that through death he might destroy the one who has the power of death, that is, the devil, and deliver all those who through fear of death were subject to lifelong slavery.

We learn something important about the devil here: he has the power of death. But what does that mean? The wording takes us back to the garden of Eden. The serpent of Eden—actually the divine being later called Satan—was cursed, cast down to the ground to (metaphorically) eat dust (Isa. 14:12; cf. Gen. 3:14). There's more here than meets the eye, though. The Hebrew word translated "ground" in Isaiah 14:12 is *erets*. This word also refers to the underworld in Old Testament theology, the realm of the dead (Ps. 71:20; Jer. 17:13; Jonah 2:7). Instead of being "like the Most High" (Isa. 14:14), God punished Satan by making him lord of the dead. Since the fall meant that all humanity inherited death (Rom. 5:12), the soul of every human being was, in effect, under the power of Satan, who holds "the power of death" according to Hebrews 2:14.

This theology is important for understanding two statements about Satan found elsewhere. Revelation 12:9 connects Satan with the serpent of Eden and describes him as "thrown down to earth." However, the reference isn't to the event of Eden because Revelation 12 further clarifies:

> Now the salvation and the power and the kingdom of our God and the authority of his Christ have come, for the accuser of our brothers has been thrown down, who accuses them day and night before our God. (Rev. 12:10)

This time the casting down coincides with the appearance of Jesus and the kingdom of God. Luke 10:18 presents the same idea. After Jesus sent out disciples who returned with the news that demons were subject to them, Jesus said, "I saw Satan fall like lightning from heaven." The messaging is profound: With the arrival of the kingdom of God (and so, believers entering that kingdom), Satan no longer had claim over their souls. Those in Christ will rise with him from death (Rom. 6:8; 2 Tim. 2:11). The power of death held by the lord of the dead was annulled.

CHAPTER 70

The Christian Life Is the Process of Becoming What You Are—and Will Be

In popular discussion, the Christian life is most often spoken of in terms like discipleship, spiritual growth, or spiritual formation. The theological term for it, drawn from the New Testament, is sanctification. The term means "holy," which is the status of being set apart for relationship with and use by God.

Sanctification is a doctrinal concept that is both "already, but not yet." According to the New Testament, every believer in Christ is already "sanctified" by being in Christ. This is why certain passages use verb tenses to speak of sanctification that give the word the feel of an already accomplished act. For example, Paul referred to the Corinthian believers (who had all sorts of spiritual problems) as "sanctified in Christ Jesus" (1 Cor. 1:2), having been "washed . . . sanctified . . . justified in the name of the Lord Jesus (1 Cor. 6:11). The writer of Hebrews told his readers that by the will of God "we have been sanctified through the offering of the body of Jesus Christ once for all" (Heb. 10:10).

However, the New Testament also describes believers as those in the process of *being* sanctified. In the very same chapter of Hebrews noted above, the writer says, "For by a single offering he has perfected for all time those who are being sanctified" (Heb. 10:14).

Peter told his readers "be holy" (1 Peter 1:16) and "grow in the grace and knowledge of our Lord and Savior Jesus Christ" (2 Peter 3:18). Paul exhorted believers to "walk in a manner worthy of the Lord, fully pleasing to him, bearing fruit in every good work" (Col. 1:10) and to "present your bodies as a living sacrifice, holy and acceptable to God" so as to "not be conformed to this world, but [to] be transformed by the renewal of your mind" (Rom. 12:1).

Sanctification is a lifelong process, and the New Testament describes it as such. Ephesians 5:26–27 informs us that Christ gave himself for the church "that he might sanctify her . . . [and] present the church to himself in splendor, without spot or wrinkle or any such thing, that she might be holy and without blemish." Paul prayed that "he who began a good work in you will bring it to completion at the day of Jesus Christ" (Phil. 1:6). Perhaps most spectacularly, John described the believer's final sanctification this way:

> See what kind of love the Father has given to us, that we should be called children of God; and so we are. . . . Beloved, we are God's children now, and what we will be has not yet appeared; but we know that when he appears we shall be like him, because we shall see him as he is. (1 John 3:1–3)

All who are already in Christ are in the process of being conformed to the image of Jesus (Rom. 8:29), who himself is the exact imprint of God's nature (Heb. 1:3), by being "transformed into the same image from one degree of glory to another" (2 Cor. 3:18).

CHAPTER 71

You Don't Have Two of You inside Your Body

I love the movie *The Princess Bride*. One of my favorite scenes is when the dead body of the lead character (Wesley, the "Man in Black") is taken by his friends to Miracle Max. After an absurd inspection of the body, Max has good news. Wesley is only "mostly dead." Max concocts a pill to bring Wesley back to life so he can get revenge on their mutual enemy. The scene is deliberately ridiculous, which is what's made it so popular and memorable. There's no such thing as being "mostly dead." You're either dead or not. Unless of course you're talking about what most Christians believe about sanctification. Then "mostly dead" makes sense (somehow).

I'm talking about the doctrinal myth that Christians still have an old nature. It's one of the most prevalent teachings about the Christian life—and one of the most misguided. Romans 6:5–7 flatly denies the idea:

> For if we have been united with him in a death like his, we shall certainly be united with him in a resurrection like his. We know that our old self was crucified with him in order that the body of sin might be brought to nothing, so that we would no longer be enslaved to sin. For one who has died has been set free from sin.

Do you see the issue? If you are united to Christ—if you are a believer—then you have died with him. Paul said, "I am crucified with Christ" (Gal. 2:20). *Your old self was crucified.* Your old self is declared here to be dead, not mostly dead, but *dead.* If anyone is in Christ, he is a new creation (2 Cor. 5:17).

So why is the notion that Christians still have the old nature inside them so common? Because we sin. Paul talked about it in the exact same passage where he described the old self crucified and dead. Look carefully at his language:

- "Our old self was crucified with him in order that *the body of sin* might be brought to nothing" (Rom. 6:6).
- "So you also must consider yourselves dead to sin and alive to God in Christ Jesus. Let not sin therefore reign *in your mortal body*, to make you obey *its passions*" (Rom. 6:11–12).

Scripture does not teach that believers still have their old nature—their original, unredeemed self—living inside them. Rather, we are redeemed souls trapped in an unredeemed body, what Paul calls "the flesh." Our earthly desires and inclinations that are contrary to our new selves are rolled up into this metaphor. In the flesh there is nothing good (Rom. 7:18). The "old man" isn't what wars against the new man, that is, the "soul" of the believer. Peter is blunt: "The passions of the flesh . . . wage war against your soul" (1 Peter 2:11). We await "the redemption of the body" because our soul is already redeemed (Rom. 8:23).

CHAPTER 72

The Divine Presence of the Tabernacle and Temple Dwells inside Believers

A lot of heavy doctrinal teaching is attached to what happens when someone believes in Jesus Christ. Our sins are forgiven (Eph. 1:7; Col. 1:14). We are placed into the body of Christ, the family of God (1 Cor. 12:12–13). We are reconciled to God (Rom. 5:10–11). We are sealed with the Holy Spirit (Eph. 1:13). Most Christians are familiar with these concepts. But in my experience, it comes as something of a shock when believers learn that the same glory that indwelt the holy of holies in both the tabernacle and the temple, the room that held the ark of the covenant, now dwells inside them.

This profound idea is one of those points of doctrine that Bible students read but can easily gloss over. Paul asked the Corinthians:

> Do you not know that you are God's temple and that God's Spirit dwells in you? If anyone destroys God's temple, God will destroy him. For God's temple is holy, and you are that temple. (1 Cor. 3:16–17)

Here Paul is emphasizing the corporate body of believers, not the individual. We know this because the verb form in verse 16 ("you are") is grammatically plural, as is the pronoun ("you") in verse 17. Collectively, the believing community is indwelt by the divine presence that indwelt the temple in the Old Testament. He reminded the Corinthians of this truth in his second letter—this time drawing the direct analogy to the Israelite temple:

> What agreement has the temple of God with idols? For we are the temple of the living God; as God said,
>
> "I will make my dwelling among them and walk
> among them,
> and I will be their God,
> and they shall be my people." (2 Cor. 6:16;
> cf. Ezek. 37:27)

But Paul wasn't finished. He turns to the individual in 1 Corinthians 6:19, where his focus (see his comment about sexual morality in the prior verse) is the believer's body: "Do you not know that your body is a temple of the Holy Spirit within you?"

These ideas are sometimes conveyed subtly. Peter employs a Greek word (*skēnōma*) used by Septuagint translators for the Hebrew word for "temple" to describe the believer's body ("the putting off of my body will be soon"; 2 Peter 1:13–14). Elsewhere Paul uses the closely related Greek word *skēnos* to describe the believer's body and his heavenly abode with the Lord:

> For we know that if the *tent* that is our earthly home is destroyed, we have a building from God, a house not made with hands, eternal in the heavens. For in this *tent* we groan, longing to put on our heavenly dwelling. (2 Cor. 5:1–2)

As shocking as it sounds, you are where God, through the Spirit, chooses to abide.

PART 8

THE BEGINNING AND END OF THE WORLD

CHAPTER 73

Genesis 1:1–3 Allows for More than One View of Creation

> In the beginning, God created the heavens and the earth. The earth was without form and void, and darkness was over the face of the deep. And the Spirit of God was hovering over the waters. And God said, "Let there be light," and there was light. (Gen. 1:1–3)

Many Bible students presume the meaning of these familiar verses is self-evident. Before there was anything, there was only God. Then God decided to create matter: the heavens and the earth as we know them. The result of the initial creation act (v. 1) was a formless and empty earth, along with a great expanse of water ("the deep"). Then God continued creating by speaking light into existence. What could be simpler?

Actually, a lot of things. Genesis 1:1–3 has naturally become a battleground because modern astronomy requires stretches of time that seem incompatible with seven twenty-four-hour days of Genesis 1. But English translations obscure Hebrew grammatical points that allow a resolution.

The very first word of the first verse presents a problem to the above meaning. This first word (*bereshit*) is actually a phrase (a preposition with a noun). Put simply, there is no definite article (the word "the") in *bereshit*. That means we should avoid using the word "the" in an English translation. The result is something like "To begin with" or "When God began to create." Without the definite article, there is no definite beginning.

The "meaning," drawn from the ESV above, presumes that the first three verses are a linear chronology of events. The Hebrew grammar actually doesn't allow for that. Like any other language, Hebrew has (grammatically) independent and dependent sentences. The former is a sentence that can stand alone, needing nothing added to convey a complete idea. The latter needs something added to express a complete thought. If we translate the first verse "When God began to create the heavens and the earth," the thought is incomplete; it needs finishing.

Additionally, verse 2 has an unseen Hebrew grammatical signal that is *designed* to *interrupt* linear sequence (called a disjunctive *waw*). That means verse 2 is a parenthetical thought to the incomplete idea of verse 1. The two verses are *not* a sequence. Rather, they are two preparatory thoughts to verse 3, which, grammatically, is the first creative act of the passage. If you read the passage that way, matter already existed before God began to work, and he essentially took that matter and made a habitable earth out of it.

There are other verses that make it clear that any matter present prior to Genesis 1:1 was still created by God (Col. 1:16). But lacking a definite time reference in Genesis 1:1–3 produces an indefinite period of time prior to God's work in verse 3.

CHAPTER 74

The Original Created Earth Was Not Eden

Sometimes the most familiar biblical themes and stories are the ones most in need of close examination. A case in point is how we think about Eden, and in this case, there are theological ramifications. When they hear the word "Eden," many Christians think immediately of the newly created *world*. I've taught more than one Bible class where students looked at me like I had two heads when I told them that the creation story *doesn't* equate the world with Eden.

The first description of Eden in the biblical text makes this obvious. Eden was clearly not the earth; it was a very small place *on* earth. Eden was marked by specific points of geography:

> Now a river flowed out from Eden that watered the garden, and from there it diverged and became four branches. The name of the first is the Pishon. It went around all the land of Havilah, where there is gold. (The gold of that land is good; bdellium and onyx stones are there.) And the name of the second is Gihon. It went around all the land of Cush. And the name of the third is Tigris. It flows east of Assyria. And the fourth river is the Euphrates. (Gen. 2:10–14)

There are other indications in the text that reinforce a distinction between Eden and the rest of the planet. Genesis 2:8 tells us that "the LORD God planted a garden in Eden, in the east." That Eden is located "in the east" places it at a location on the earth; it therefore cannot be the earth.

Lastly, Eden and the earth must be distinct since Adam and Eve are expelled from it and have to live elsewhere. Unless we're going to say Adam and Eve were shot into outer space, Eden and the planet earth must be distinct.

Why bring up the topic? Mainly because when Bible students talk about creation they regularly make claims about it that can only be said of Eden. For example: "God's original creation was perfect." Only Eden deserved such a description. First, it was the dwelling place of God, and so the presumption that the environment was perfect *in this one place on earth* is reasonable. Second, Adam and Eve were tasked with "subduing" the earth, which is something they were not commanded to do to Eden. Eden didn't need subjugation, but there was something about the rest of the planet that needed taming or restraint. Lastly, the fact that the earth needed to be filled implies that it was lacking things that God wanted for it. If God's initial creation had been flawless, it would not be lacking in anything.

The way Christians conceive and talk about creation influences the way we think about science. Certainly, science is not omniscient, but sometimes we might be dismissing truth God intends us to see in the natural world when we think imprecisely about the original earth.

CHAPTER 75

The Bible Does Not Rule Out Death before the Fall

Earlier we talked about how familiar passages can produce assumptions in our thinking, using the example of how Eden was not the entire earth. We're going to look at the creation story again, but this time we'll start in the New Testament.

Romans 5:12 is a verse that gets pressed into service for several doctrinal ideas, those coherent and those flawed. One instance of the latter is the notion that this verse teaches there was no such thing as death prior to the sin of Adam in Eden.

> So then, just as sin entered the world through one man and death through sin, and so death spread to all people with the result that all sinned. (NET)*

Look at the verse closely. An incongruity between what it says and the idea that there was no death before the fall should become apparent. The text very plainly and explicitly restricts the spread of death resulting from Adam's sin to *human beings*: "so death spread to all people." What happened at the fall resulted in a transition from there being no death among humankind to death being a

* The translation of the last part of the verse ("with the result that all sinned") is found in the scholarly translation notes that accompany the NET Bible.

reality for humankind. The verse says nothing about whether there could have been death before the fall outside the human race (e.g., the death of plants, animals, microbes).

The implications of simply allowing this verse to say what it says are significant. For example, in the debates that rage between various factions of creationism, one recurring claim is that any view of creationism that doesn't explain fossils by means of a global flood cannot have biblical support because there can be no death prior to the fall. There is no need to further suppose that carnivorous dinosaurs like Tyrannosaurus rex were originally plant eaters before the fall. Romans 5:12 does not speak to animal death (and no other verse makes such a case). Consequently, turning it into a commentary on paleontology is terribly misguided.

Here's the lesson: let Scripture speak. We ought not speak for Scripture. Avoiding that temptation will save us from some embarrassing ideas. It will also open our minds to new interpretive possibilities that are grounded in the inspired text.

CHAPTER 76

The Church Isn't Absent from the Book of Revelation

Any doctrine of end times is driven by presuppositions brought to the book of Revelation. By "presuppositions" I mean *decisions* made about *how* the book is to be understood before ever reading the book. Two assumptions that many Christians have about the book is that (1) the church is absent from the book's description of the tribulation period (Rev. 4–18) and (2) this absence is due to the removal of the church in Revelation 4:1 in a rapture. Since the first assumption is demonstrably incorrect, the second assumption cannot be sustained.

It is true that the last occurrence of the word *ekklēsia* ("church") in Revelation prior to its ending benediction (Rev. 22:16) occurs in Revelation 3:22, the final verse of chapter three. In Revelation 4:1, John writes, "After this I looked, and behold, a door standing open in heaven! And the first voice, which I had heard speaking to me like a trumpet, said, 'Come up here, and I will show you what must take place after this.'" This trumpet sound and command to "come up" is taken as a description of the rapture, which accounts for the absence of the word *ekklēsia* in the rest of the book.

The problem with this assumption is that believers in the New Testament are referred to collectively with other words besides *ekklēsia*. One of the most common is the word "saints" (*hagioi*).

This plural term often describes believers of the church (e.g., Acts 9:13, 32, 41; 26:10; Rom. 8:27; 12:13; 15:25–26; 2 Cor. 8:4; Eph. 3:8; 4:12; Jude 3). Paul opens many of his letters to churches with the word to greet believers (e.g., Rom. 1:7; 1 Cor. 1:2; 2 Cor. 1:1; Eph. 1:1; Phil. 1:1; Col. 1:2).

This same plural term occurs several times after Revelation 4:1 to describe believers on earth during the events described in Revelation 4–18. For example, the beast "makes war on the saints" (Rev. 13:7), prompting John to call for the "endurance and faith of the saints" (Rev. 13:10; cf. 14:12). The enemies of God's people "have shed the blood of the saints" (Rev. 16:6). The great harlot, mystery Babylon, is "drunk with the blood of the saints" (Rev. 17:6). That indictment is repeated in Revelation 18:24 where the saints are included in the long history of the people of God who have been "slain on the earth."

There is little ambiguity here. The vocabulary for the church, the believing community and the body of Christ, used widely throughout the New Testament, occurs in the book of Revelation after the fourth chapter. The notion that the church is absent is demonstrably wrong, so Revelation 4:1 is no indication of a rapture. That doctrinal idea is of course debated in relation to several other passages and issues. But Revelation 4:1 and the flawed assumption that goes with it cannot be called into service to make the case for a rapture.

CHAPTER 77

Which Wrath Are We Talking About?

We've already talked about the doctrine of the rapture, the idea that believers are removed from the earth sometime during the end times. According to this doctrinal idea, the church is removed before God's wrath is poured out on the earth in the tribulation period. These two assumptions are problematic. The church is, in some way, a new Israel, and the church isn't removed from the awful events described in the book of Revelation. Nevertheless, there are passages that seem to teach that believers are removed from the tribulation period:

> Your faith in God has gone forth everywhere, so that we need not say anything. For they themselves report concerning us the kind of reception we had among you, and how you turned to God from idols to serve the living and true God, and to wait for his Son from heaven, whom he raised from the dead, Jesus *who delivers us from the wrath to come.* (1 Thess. 1:8–10)

Because the doctrine of a rapture is so prevalent in contemporary popular evangelical thinking, it's easy to read this verse and presume that what Paul is describing in this letter is a time or terrible upheaval in the end times. But Paul never actually says that. It's true, though, that Paul mentions the second coming of Jesus ("wait for his Son from heaven"). But in terms of biblical theology, there is another wrath from which believers will be delivered when Jesus returns: the final judgment and the second death, which is eternal separation from God.

Later in the same letter Paul writes this:

> But since we belong to the day, let us be sober, having put on the breastplate of faith and love, and for a helmet the hope of salvation. For *God has not destined us for wrath, but to obtain salvation* through our Lord Jesus Christ. (1 Thess. 5:8–9)

Paul's description here seems to connect the idea of future wrath to the final judgment (the "great white throne" judgment) described in passages like Revelation 20:11–15, where the dead are judged according to whether they are found in the book of life (v. 12). If not, they face the wrath of the lake of fire (v. 15). This is consistent with verses like John 3:36: "Whoever believes in the Son has eternal life; whoever does not obey the Son shall not see life, but the wrath of God remains on him" (cf. Rom. 5:9).

The point is that 1 Thessalonians 1:8–10 does not clearly speak of believers being removed from earth before the tribulation. The point might be that believers are saved from final wrath. Consequently, care must be taken to not prop up end times doctrine on its "wrath" language.

CHAPTER 78

The Old and New Testaments Differ on the Details of the Afterlife, Not the Destinations

We're all going to die. Everyone does. If I ask you what happens to believers and unbelievers after death, the odds are high you'll think of heaven and hell. That's understandable since the Bible devotes a lot of attention to the afterlife. But if you've ever read the Old Testament carefully, you've probably come away with the impression that there's a lot less afterlife talk in it than the New Testament. If so, you'd be correct, and scholars have taken note. Many believe that the Old Testament never really speaks of either a heaven or hell.

The Old Testament theology of an afterlife is dominated by the word *sheol*, which occurs over sixty times. In many instances *sheol* refers to the grave, the place all humans go (Ps. 89:48), whether they're righteous (Gen. 37:35; 42:38; 44:31) or wicked (Job 24:19; Ps. 9:17; Prov. 5:1–5). Once people die, they tend to stay dead, so *sheol* can also refer to the place where the dead remain, the afterlife (Job 7:9; Isa. 14:9). And since the bones of the dead were interred in the ground, *sheol*—the underworld realm of the dead—was considered to be located somewhere deep in the earth. People went "down" to *sheol* (Job 7:9; 21:13; Prov. 7:27).

The Old Testament therefore seems to speak of the afterlife in "equal" terms—it's a place all the dead go, contrary to the dramatically oppositional destinations of heaven and hell described in the New Testament. While the Old Testament lacks the afterlife detail of the New, the equality above is overstated. The Old Testament does speak of a blissful hope for the righteous in the afterlife. But we really can't discern that if we focus on the word *sheol*. The hope of the righteous was that God would take them out of *sheol* to be in his presence.

In Old Testament theology, God could remove people from *sheol* (Ps. 30:3; 49:15). Contemplating death, the psalmist says,

> Nevertheless, I am continually with you;
> you hold my right hand. . . .
> Afterward you will receive me to glory. . . .
> God is the strength of my heart and my portion
> forever. (Ps. 73:23–24, 26)

The "holding of the hand" deserves some attention, since "upholding" is elsewhere associated with the presence of God:

> But you have upheld me because of my integrity,
> and set me in your presence forever. (Ps. 41:12)

In Psalm 16:10–11 David wrote,

> For you will not abandon my soul to Sheol,
> or let your holy one see corruption.
> You make known to me the path of life;
> in your presence there is fullness of joy;
> at your right hand are pleasures *forevermore*.

Clearly, the expectation of those faithful to Yahweh was to be with the Lord and not remain in *sheol*.

It's a good thing, too. The alternative, being left in *sheol*, meant staying dead in a place also inhabited by the departed spirits of the dead giants, the enemies of Israel (Job 26:5–6; Prov. 9:18; Isa. 14:9; cf. Deut. 2:11; 1 Chron. 20:4). While the Old Testament never describes everlasting torment, death was permanent and frightening for the unbeliever. Only in the Lord's presence could life be again experienced.

CHAPTER 79

There's More than One Way to Understand Eternal Punishment

Many Christians presume that the doctrine of hell, though horrific, has been uncontroversial in the history of Christianity. They assume that believers since the time of the apostles have all basically held the same view. That isn't the case.

The dominant view of hell for two millennia of Christian history is that eternal punishment means unending conscious torment for the unbeliever. The Old Testament contains no evidence for this idea. Instead, death remains permanent. The real issue, though, is what the New Testament says on the matter. It may surprise you, but there's more than one way to understand its language about hell. Conscious torment may be more familiar, but the everlasting judgment of hell may refer to the permanent (everlasting) extinction of unbelievers.

For example, the description of unquenchable fire where "the worm does not die" (Mark 9:43, 48) is a quotation of Isaiah 66:24, which describes a flame that consumes the *dead corpses* of those judged at the day of the Lord. The context of the entire chapter is the eschatological judgment of the wicked who are "slain" by God with fire and sword (Isa. 66:16) and "meet their end" (Isa. 66:17). In contrast, the righteous "will endure." The idea of the unquenched fire, then, may refer to the fact that God's judgment cannot be stopped and is inescapable. The imagery of maggots ("worms") speaks to the unstoppable consumption of the corpse as well.

Revelation 14:11 refers to the final divine judgment and says, "The smoke of their torment goes up forever and ever." It's easy to see how this verse can support conscious torment, but the same phrasing in the Old Testament clearly speaks to the finality of life extinction. In Isaiah 34:9–10 we read about God's judgment of Edom:

> Her land shall become burning pitch.
> Night and day it shall not be quenched;
> its smoke shall go up forever.

Obviously, Edom isn't still burning.

Another important verse is Revelation 20:14, perhaps the most difficult verse for those who want to hold the traditional view of eternal conscious torment: "Then Death and Hades were thrown into the lake of fire. This is the second death, the lake of fire." This echoes Paul's statement that "The last enemy to be destroyed is death" (1 Cor. 15:26). How can hell be eternal when death is done away with? Perhaps the point is the finality of death for all unbelievers—in contrast to life eternal for those who believe.

CHAPTER 80

The Return of Jesus Was at Hand Two Thousand Years Ago—Just like It Is Now

The New Testament writers believed the return of Jesus would occur in their lifetime. Some used the term "at hand" to express that assumption. This phrase has, in our time, been interpreted in various ways and, not surprisingly, produced controversy among Christians.

Many Christians take note of passages that say "the end of all things is at hand" (1 Peter 4:7) or "the coming of the Lord is at hand" (James 5:8) and presume that the return of Jesus is imminent, that it could happen at any moment. The fact that these phrases were written two thousand years ago doesn't deter that understanding, but encourages it. The reasoning is that surely, after two millennia, Jesus could indeed return at any moment.

The idea of Jesus's imminent return isn't completely coherent. For example, Jesus's parables (Luke 19:11–27; Matt. 24:45–51; 25:5, 19) suggest a period of delay. Of course, we've had two thousand years of delay, but if the "at hand" statements are still viable, how are we to assume the delays implied in the parables are about to end?

More significant is the fact that Jesus taught that the gospel would be preached to all nations (Matt. 24:14) and the temple would be destroyed before he would return (Matt. 24:2). The second event is of course known history. The first is not; it's subject to interpretation. Has the gospel reached every people? I would suggest it isn't a stretch to say no, it hasn't.

New Testament writers understood the teaching of Matthew 24:14 as related to the Old Testament theology that the nations would be brought back into the fold of the people of God (Isa. 66:20–23). The nations had been disinherited at Babel, and Israel was created thereafter. Israel alone were the people of God, but Israel would be the key to reaching the others (Gen. 12:3). Paul taught that "a partial hardening has come upon Israel, until the fullness of the gentiles has come in" (Rom. 11:25). The verse points to the idea that Jesus would not return until the full number of gentiles from all the disinherited nations had been brought into the family of God. Since the gospel had been taken to the gentiles (Acts 11:1–18), particularly with respect to Paul's ministry (Acts 13:46–48), it's no wonder that the disciples and New Testament writers thought the Lord would return at any moment.

We're still waiting for the Lord to return, and there are many who have not yet heard the gospel. The New Testament never assigns a number that defines "the fullness of the gentiles," so the timing of the second coming isn't definite. The Lord could return at any moment, when God decides the full allotment of the gentiles. Our situation is basically identical to that of the apostles. Instead of speaking of the Lord's return as "imminent," I'd suggest that the word "impending" better captures both circumstances—theirs and ours.